Teacher's Survival Guide

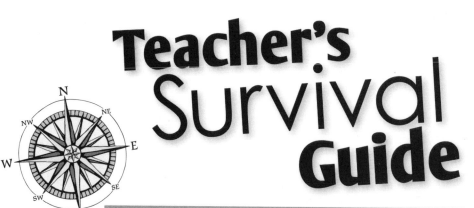

Differentiating Instruction in the Elementary Classroom

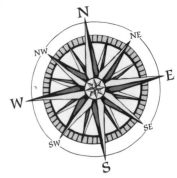

acher's Survival Guide

Differentiating Instruction in the Elementary Classroom

**Julia Link Roberts, Ed.D., and
Tracy Ford Inman, Ed.D.**

PRUFROCK PRESS INC.
WACO, TEXAS

Library of Congress Cataloging-in-Publication Data

Roberts, Julia L. (Julia Link)
 Teacher's survival guide : differentiating instruction in the elementary classroom / by Julia Link Roberts and Tracy Ford Inman.
   p. cm.
 ISBN 978-1-59363-979-2 (pbk.)
 1. Individualized instruction. 2. Education, Elementary. I. Inman, Tracy F. (Tracy Ford), 1963- II. Title.
 LB1031.R58 2013
 371.39'4--dc23

2012033158

Edited by Lacy Compton

Layout design by Raquel Trevino

ISBN-13: 978-1-59363-979-2

Printed in the United States of America.

At the time of this book's publication, all facts and figures cited are the most current available. All telephone numbers, addresses, and website URLs are accurate and active. All publications, organizations, websites, and other resources exist as described in the book, and all have been verified. The authors and Prufrock Press Inc. make no warranty or guarantee concerning the information and materials given out by organizations or content found at websites, and we are not responsible for any changes that occur after this book's publication. If you find an error, please contact Prufrock Press Inc.

Prufrock Press Inc.
P.O. Box 8813
Waco, TX 76714-8813
Phone: (800) 998-2208
Fax: (800) 240-0333
http://www.prufrock.com

Table of Contents

1 Differentiation: The Basics

Learning how to learn is life's most important skill.

—Tony Buzan

Key Question

- What must be in place to motivate teachers to differentiate instruction?

The goal of school is for all children to learn on an ongoing basis. Developing lifelong learners must be the priority at all schools and, consequently, for all educators—classroom teachers, specials teachers, counselors, and school leaders.

The Goals of Differentiation

The goals of differentiation are complementary to the goals for school:

1. Every student will make *continuous progress* no matter how old she is or at what levels her knowledge and skills are as she begins the unit of study.

2. Every student will become a *lifelong learner*, the long-term goal for all children and young people. Learning at the appropriate level of challenge is motivating and builds lifelong learners.

These goals are important at each stage of K–12 education, and they are especially important as children begin their formal schooling. A great start in school means that children are enjoying learning. That love of learning happens in classrooms in which children are respected as learners and are engaged in learning on a daily basis. Differentiation is planned to allow for growth in learning capacity. Differentiation increases interest in learning and hones skills for learners. Lifelong learning is the long-term goal of education.

Continuous progress means that everyone has the opportunity to learn regardless of readiness level; whether a weakness needs to be shored up or a strength needs to be developed; a child's reading level is at, above, or below grade level; whatever the student's interests are for the content being studied; or whether the student is an English language learner or native English speaker. Everyone learns when the teacher recognizes differences among children, respects those differences, and accommodates them to engage children in learning.

Definition of Differentiation

Definitions of *differentiation* are numerous. For this book, the definition of differentiation is tied to the match—the match of the curriculum and learning experiences to learners. A teacher who differentiates effectively matches the content (basic to complex), the level of the thinking processes, the sophistication and choice of the product, and/or the assessment to the student or cluster of students. Differentiation is not a strategy but rather a way of teaching that accommodates differences among children so that all are learning on an ongoing basis.

Rationale for Differentiation

Response to Differences

The most basic reason to differentiate is that children differ. Because children are different in their readiness to learn specific content and skills, it is necessary to respond accordingly. Children of the same age who are in the same grade have a range of reading abilities, varied interests and experiences with the content being studied, and different levels of skills for thinking critically and creatively as well as in communicating via writing and speaking. Children seldom come to any class ready for learning at the identical rate and at the same level of complexity.

Figure 1. A fairy tale. Illustration by J. W. Bellemere.

As Figure 1 suggests, it is fiction or a fairy tale to assume that all children in a class are at the same level such that a one-size-fits-all lesson will allow all of them to make continuous progress. One lesson for all children will likely be too difficult for a few and not challenging enough to hold the interest of or challenge others.

A Standard of Excellence

For our communities to thrive, elementary, middle, and high schools must be centered on a standard of excellence. A standard of excellence means that all children achieve at levels that are challenging—but not so challenging that they are not attainable. Grade-level learning experiences will provide the correct match for many children at a particular grade level but not for all. All learning experiences for a particular age group will not "fit" all children appropriately any more than one size of shoes will offer the proper fit for all children who are in the second grade or fifth grade. No child should be held back or inappropriately challenged because she is a particular age; rather, learning opportunities must be matched to the children.

Excellence, then, should be a personal standard rather than a grade-level standard. A standard of excellence means that each child makes at least a year's growth in achievement no matter what the starting point for the school year. More than one year of achievement would be even better, and such growth in achievement is quite possible. However, it is unacceptable in a school that is centered on excellence for any child to make less than a year of progress. That includes children whose achievement level is above or way above the grade that they are in just as it includes children who are not yet achieving at grade level.

All children need ongoing opportunities to learn at the highest level at which they can achieve. Learning at an advanced level is certainly within the realm of possibility for a much higher percentage of children than currently are achieving at advanced levels. *Mind the (Other) Gap!* (Plucker, Burroughs, & Song, 2010) described the excellence gap as the "difference between subgroups of students performing at the highest level of achievement" (p. 1). The report stated:

> That excellence gaps have received so little attention over the past decade is a major oversight. The existence of such gaps raises doubts about the success of federal and state governments in providing greater and more equitable education opportunities, particularly as the proportion of minority and low-income students continues to rise. The goal of guaranteeing that all children will have the opportunity to reach their academic potential is called into question if educational policies only assist some students while others are left behind. Furthermore, the comparatively small percentage of students scoring at the highest level on achievement tests suggests that children with advanced academic potential are being under-served, with potentially serious consequences for the long-term economic competiveness of the U.S. (p. 1)

Focus on the achievement gaps among children from lower income families, children from various racial and ethnic groups, and children with special education needs has been on reaching proficiency. Many of these children are capable of reaching advanced levels (because high-ability and gifted children come from all backgrounds), but currently that is not the emphasis in many schools and classrooms.

Fairness

Is it fair for different children to be learning at different levels in one classroom? Definitely. It is unfair to have some children struggling with assignments that are too difficult, just as it is unfair to have some children waiting for something new to learn. Fairness means matching learning experiences to needs. Although it is not the usual way to think about needs, it is important to remember that needs are created from strengths as well as deficits. Needs also arise from the pace at which children learn. Some students need more time and multiple opportunities to practice a skill or to learn the content, while others need less time and few repetitions (or perhaps no repetition) to master a skill or to learn the content. Fairness means allowing each child opportunities to learn new things every school day. Fairness means matching the level of complexity and the pace of learning to the child's readiness, interest in the concept or topic, and/or learning profile. Ward (1983) stated,

> One of the objectives of free public education in a democracy is to provide equal opportunity for all youth to develop their potential abilities to the fullest. In attempting to reach this objective educators have come to the realization that *equal* opportunity does not mean *identical* opportunity. (p. 1)

Ward (1980) coined the term *differential learning* to describe the concept that is now known as *differentiated instruction*.

Differentiation: Not Really a New Concept

Perhaps the best place to start to examine differentiation is with early school practices that differentiated instruction for learners. In rural America, effective teachers in the one-room schoolhouse arranged lessons by grouping children by ability (not by age), so that all children were learning—but not the same thing at the same time. *Understood Betsy* (Fisher, 1917), a novel about a 9-year-old girl, describes her puzzlement as she moves from a school organized by grades to a one-room school. There she finds that the teacher has her reading with the seventh graders, doing arithmetic with the second graders, and spelling with the third graders. When Betsy remarks that she doesn't know what grade she is in, the teacher said,

> *You* aren't any grade at all, no matter where you are in school. You're just yourself, aren't you? What difference does it make what grade you're in? And what's the use of your reading little baby things too easy for you just because you don't know your multiplication table? (pp. 101–102)

Very succinctly, the teacher told Betsy why it is necessary to differentiate instruction for her if she is to learn as much as she can learn that year. The teacher understood that Betsy was an outstanding reader but was at grade level in spelling and perhaps a bit below in arithmetic. To have Betsy working at the third-grade level in all of the content areas would be holding her back in her reading for no good reason at all. Differentiation becomes very important in order to enhance students' strengths while working on learning on a daily basis.

Later, schools were organized based on the age of the child, and, although this arrangement may be efficient for organizing children, it is not a very effective way to organize children for learning when it is adhered to rigidly. Grouping by age results in a wide range of learning differences in each content area in a classroom. Some children will soar, while others are held back in a heterogeneous class in which the teacher does not differentiate instruction. Other children are pushed too hard if accommodations are not made to make the content more basic and to slow the pace, while others are lulled into complacency when there is a one-size-fits-all curriculum and pace for instruction. Either situation gets in the way of children learning on an ongoing basis, and it clouds the question of whether children even want to come to school.

Perhaps the ideal situation would be to have tutors for students. A tutor tailors lessons to meet the needs of one student. No doubt, it would be helpful to have the one-on-one relationship that a tutor has; however, that suggestion is not practical for schools. Parent or community volunteers can be used when such a relationship is needed for students to demonstrate their reading ability or to discuss interests related to what they are learning. Obviously, tutors cannot be available to deliver instruction to all children today, but differentiation can make it possible for all children to learn on an ongoing basis. Differentiation allows all children to learn and make continuous progress in a classroom.

Spelling: How to Differentiate a Lesson

Spelling provides an example of a content area that can be differentiated easily. The goal for teaching spelling is for children to learn to spell or to become better spellers. If on the Monday preassessment, a child can spell all of the words for the week and another cannot spell any of them correctly, the lesson offers no challenge for one and perhaps too much challenge for another. A differentiated spelling lesson would offer an appropriate level of challenge to each child. Without differentiation, the child who knows all or most of the words already will not really be learning any spelling unless he is given a different list of words. Spelling is a good way to examine differentiation and to begin to think about what differentiation really is and is not.

Is it appropriate differentiation to give Matilda (who can spell the words correctly on Monday) puzzles to solve while other children work on their spelling? No, that strategy is not making Matilda a better speller—the very reason that spelling is in the curriculum. Working puzzles or doing anything other than learning vocabulary words the child does not already know how to spell and use correctly is merely putting the child into a holding pattern with spelling. No one enjoys being put into a holding pattern on a plane, and the same can be said about learning. Such a situation in school creates frustrated or lazy learners.

Is it best practice to give Matilda a different list of spelling words for the week? Yes, it is, but the "catch" is that the different list must have an appropriate level of challenge for the child. Tamara Fisher (2012) wrote the following scenario, which illustrated why it is not enough for the spelling list to be different.

> I had a conversation with a fourth grader the other day and was asking her about her Spelling words. Having spent a little time in her classroom, I'd noticed that the kids took a pre-test on the list and, for whichever of those words they spelled correctly on the pre-test, they got to pick new words from a "shopping list." But the shopping list words didn't seem that much more challenging to me.
>
> Marianne agreed and said, "Yeah, I was still getting 100%'s on the final tests, too, and not needing to study the shopping list words much, either. But then Mrs. Shazam started pre-testing me on the shopping list words, also, and she found a bunch of 7th grade words that I could pick from instead."
>
> I asked her if the words from this "alternative alternative" were more challenging and she enthusiastically agreed, "Yes, I have to study now!" I asked how she was doing on her spelling tests now and she said, "Well, I'm still usually getting 100%'s, but I have to work for them now." I asked her which 100%'s were more satisfying, the piece-of-cake ones, or the ones she had to work for. "Oh, the ones I have to study for!" she said with a huge smile. "I'm learning new words, now." (para. 9–11)

Some Kids Will Need an Alternative Alternative!

Is it possible that the fourth-grade spelling list is too difficult for a fourth grader? Yes, that possibility exists, so the list of words may need to be pared back to a reasonable level of difficulty/complexity for some students. How does the teacher know if the grade-level spelling list is an appropriate match for students? Preassessment is the key. Results of the pretest must inform instructional decisions. Pretest results tell the teacher which children need extra support and perhaps a different spelling list just as they inform the teacher who needs an alternative list to enhance the difficulty and complexity of the words. All children need to be improving their spelling mastery to become better spellers.

Does it take more time for the teacher to differentiate the spelling list? Yes, but the time spent on creating new spelling lists is minimal. The results are exciting as every child is engaged in learning new words—words that are not too hard and not too easy. Differentiation creates classrooms in which children are engaged in learning. If a teacher is concerned about how to check the spelling on Friday if lists differ, that is easy, too. A child can read the list to another child or children to assess for accuracy, and then they can read the list for others with a different list. Such assessment can be low key and speedily accomplished.

Differentiation: Where Is It Happening or Not Happening?

The Regular Classroom Practices With Gifted Students study (Archambault et al., 1993) indicated that most of the more than 7,000 third- and fourth-grade teachers surveyed reported that they did not differentiate within their classrooms to address the needs of gifted students. This study included teachers in public and private schools, teachers in classrooms with various ethnic concentrations, and classrooms in rural, urban, and suburban communities as well as in various regions of the country. Westberg and Daoust (2003) replicated the study 10 years later and reported that "teachers' differentiation practices in third and fourth grade classrooms have not changed in the last 10 years" (p. 3). Such survey results present a bleak picture of differentiation for advanced learners. Table 1 presents data from the Teaching, Empowering, Leading and Learning Survey (TELL Survey), in which teachers surveyed in specific states in 2011–2012 voiced their interest in learning more about special education, gifted education, and differentiation.

The data suggest that teachers continue to want and need professional development that addresses differentiation and provides information and strategies for ensuring that children with special education needs thrive in school. These children include those with disabilities and those with gifts and talents.

Reasons Teachers Do and Do Not Differentiate

It is interesting to see what reasons teachers give for why they do and do not differentiate. When asked why they do differentiate, teachers' answers tend to focus on the students, while the opposite occurs when teachers are asked why they do not differentiate—those answers often center on teachers themselves.

Reasons educators differentiate are to address the needs of learners in a class, to maximize achievement for all students, and to develop lifelong learners. These reasons sound like motherhood and apple pie. Who would not support

Table 1
Results of the 2011–2012 TELL Survey

State and Number (Percent) of Teachers Who Completed Survey (2011–2012)	Needing Professional Development to Teach Gifted/Talented Students Effectively	Needing Professional Development to Teach Special Education Students Effectively	Needing Professional Development for Effective Differentiation of Instruction
Colorado n = 29,466 (46.78%)	n = 25,057 (57%)	n = 25,191 (56%)	n = 25,172 (56%)
Kentucky n = 42,025 (80.32%)	n = 36,092 (53%)	n = 36,307 (56%)	n = 36,299 (62%)
Maryland n = 45,902 (51.88%)	n = 32,845 (52%)	n = 33,309 (59%)	n = 33,102 (51%)
Massachusetts (2012) n = 42,404 (52.41%)	n = 36,589 (60%)	n = 36,600 (60%)	n = 36,624 (55%)
North Carolina (2012) n = 100,042 (86.22%)	n = 84,569 (47%)	n = 85,150 (52%)	n = 85,277 (54%)
Tennessee n = 57,391 (76.99%)	n = 49,426 (57%)	n = 50,110 (61%)	n = 50,027 (65%)

Note. From New Teacher Center, 2011a, 2011b, 2011c, 2011d, 2012a, 2012b. Each column shows the percentage of responding teachers who viewed the survey item as being important.

them? Yet if the reasons to differentiate are so compelling, why doesn't differentiation happen more?

The barriers to differentiation are numerous. The first, and perhaps the most cumbersome, barrier is that teachers do not have experiences with differentiation. They do not have role models to build on. Classes in which they were learners were not differentiated, so they lack experience in differentiated learning. Therefore, they need professional development on differentiation strategies.

The myth that children with gifts and talents will "make it" on their own provides an excuse for many teachers to dismiss the need for differentiation for advanced students in their classrooms. If teachers believe that advanced learners will be okay without the extra planning required to differentiate, they likely will stick to grade-level instruction and make a few modifications for children who need more time and more basic content to learn what is expected at the grade level at which they are teaching. Those modifications help some children learn but ignore the needs of children who have mastered grade-level standards.

Another reason that differentiation has not become a priority in many schools relates to the emphasis that has been placed on proficiency. Although there is a push for proficiency as the goal in many schools, Farkas and Duffett (2010) stated:

> Teachers want these advanced (some say "gifted" or "gifted and talented") students to move up the list of education priorities because educating them properly is the thing to do and because it's good for the nation, but mostly because they see in their own classrooms youngsters whose considerable talents are not adequately challenged or utilized. (p. 50)

This study indicates that teachers know that they should be ensuring continuous progress for their advanced students even when the emphasis in their schools has been on reaching proficiency. Proficiency is an admirable goal if you have not reached it; however, it is no goal at all for children who have attained proficiency or beyond.

Differentiation: What It Is and What It Isn't

Perhaps a good way to answer the question of what is differentiation is to begin by answering what differentiation is not.
- Differentiation is not just different.
- Differentiation is not just offering choice.
- Differentiation is not just doing what the class does plus more or less work.
- Differentiation is not the same as individualized instruction. Individualizing instruction would be very difficult in a classroom with 20 or more students.

Differentiation is *different with a purpose*, and learning experiences should be at an appropriate level of difficulty for the learners. Yes, differentiated learning experiences are matched to readiness, interests, and learning profile. Differentiation is learner centered. The teacher adjusts instruction to make certain that it is not so difficult that one or more children are frustrated, nor is it so easy that one or more children can complete the assignment without much effort. Jason Johans, a teacher in the Greenbriar County Schools, WV, compares differentiation to pitching and batting.

> I liken the teacher in the classroom to a pitcher at a baseball game, and the students are the batters. It is our job to set up the information in a way that will allow for students to knock it out of the park, so to speak. We don't want to make it too easy and lob the information right over the plate. We also don't want to make it too hard, causing the student to "strike out." We want to throw a couple curves at them to make them do their own thinking, so they will eventually see it coming and score a run for the home team. (personal communication, April 29, 2012)

It is important that the curriculum is within a child's zone of proximal development. Vygotsky (1978) defined this zone as the "distance between the actual developmental level as determined by independent problem solving and the level of potential development as determined through problem solving under adult guidance or in collaboration with more capable peers" (p. 86). For a classroom teacher, the zone of proximal development is crucial to understand if children are to be appropriately challenged. As described in the analogy of differentiation and the baseball game, the appropriate match with children and the curriculum must include challenge, but not so much challenge that it produces frustration—the goal is for them to reach to make it to the next level of learning.

The Basic Steps in Differentiation

There are three basic steps in differentiation: planning, preassessing, and differentiating the learning experience. Questions guide each of the three steps (Roberts & Inman, 2009b):

1. *Planning Question*: What do I want students to know, understand, and be able to do?
2. *Preassessment Question*: Who already knows, understands, and/or can use the content or demonstrate the skills? Who needs additional support in order to know, understand, and/or demonstrate the skills?
3. *Differentiation Question*: What can I do for him, her, or them so they can make continuous progress and extend their learning? (p. 9)

The starting point for effective differentiation must be planning. It is not possible to move to the second step, preassessment, without the teacher establishing what the students are to know, understand, and be able to do at the conclusion of the unit of study—the end goals of the unit. Good planning is essential in effective differentiation. Only after establishing the end goals or objectives can the teacher assess students to see if learning the content or mastering the skills is too much of a stretch for the child or if there is no stretch at all, as the student already knows most of the content and has mastered the skills. Differentiation is appropriate in both cases: The student needs differentiated learning experiences to receive additional support or he needs differentiated learning experiences to ensure that the content is complex enough to be challenging and the pace is rapid enough to maintain his interest.

Ongoing assessment allows teachers to determine what students know and are able to do in relation to the topic or concept being studied. The next step in differentiation is to match learning experiences to children's and young people's readiness and interests in relation to the topic or concept as well as their learning profiles. Children learn when they are engaged in learning at an appropriately challenging level—not too hard and not too easy. That match is the essential ingredient in effective differentiation.

An Overview of This Survival Guide on Differentiation

This book is planned to provide essential information on differentiating instruction for elementary children. It is intended for teachers new to differentiation, whether they are new to teaching or experienced teachers. This first chapter provides the foundation for the model in Chapter 2. The Effective Differentiation Model shows the relationship of various components in a differentiated classroom. Subsequent chapters describe content, process, products, and assessment as dimensions to differentiate for learners; how to establish a learning environment that supports differentiation; and management strategies to enhance differentiated learning. Also included are chapters describing sample strategies that differentiate, ways to meet the Common Core State Standards while differentiating, and how technology can be used to enhance differentiation in an elementary classroom. Each chapter also includes survival tips and a survival toolkit containing useful print and electronic resources. Survival is important for teachers to think about as they embark upon a journey into differentiation. If it were really easy to differentiate, all teachers would be doing so. The book is written for teachers who want the goals of maintaining continuous progress for all students and developing lifelong learners to characterize their teaching. It will be the handbook for starting to differentiate, providing the guidance to persist in differentiating, and encouraging teachers as they build a repertoire of strategies to differentiate in their classrooms.

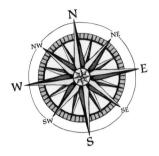

Survival Tips

- It may be a great step to get your grade-level team or a group of teachers (the entire staff would be ideal) to engage in a study of differentiation. This book may be your starting point with a book study.

- Interview parents and students about ways to learn that are most engaging (enjoyable for the students). This information would be especially important with parents of students who need extra support and those who already know some, even most, of the content and skills expected for the grade level.

- Think about the definition of differentiation in this chapter and the three questions that are essential for defensible differentiation. How might you get colleagues (grade-level teachers or the faculty) discussing differentiation and routinely posing and answering the three essential questions in their planning?

Survival Toolkit

- Carol Tomlinson on Differentiation: Proactive Instruction (http://www.youtube.com/watch?v=mpy6rDnXNbs): This talk by Dr. Carol Tomlinson provides insight into differentiation—the rationale and basics for differentiating in classrooms. Invite your colleagues to watch with you.

- Hot Topic: Differentiation of Curriculum and Instruction (http://www.nagc.org/index2.aspx?id=978): On this page of the National Association for Gifted Children (NAGC) website, there is an overview of reasons to differentiate and links to resources.

2 Key Components of Effective Differentiation

Differentiation isn't a fad. Differentiation isn't a trend. Differentiation isn't an invitation. Differentiation is meeting the needs of our students. Differentiation is doing what is best for our students. Differentiation is an expectation.

—Kimberly Hewitt and Daniel Weckstein

Key Question

- What components of instruction can be modified to make differentiation effective and defensible?

If all second graders came into the classroom in the fall reading at the same level or equally adept at understanding mathematics, there would be no reason to differentiate instruction. However, that is not the case, as children enter classrooms at a variety of levels of readiness. Consequently, it is essential for teachers to differentiate instruction so all children will learn on an ongoing basis and so that each child will be learning the skills and experiencing the joys of being a lifelong learner.

Differentiation has several dimensions that combine to make the instruction effective. As educators begin their journey into differentiation, it is vital that they understand the components. Each component of the Effective Differentiation

Model: An Instructional Model to Support Continuous Progress and Lifelong Learning (EDM; see Figure 2) will be discussed here as well as in subsequent chapters in greater detail.

The Learner

The primary reasons for instructional planning and for differentiation are to ensure that learners make continuous progress and become lifelong learners. Everything about learning must have the learner as the core consideration. Primary factors that are important to consider about the learners are (a) their readiness to learn the specific content or concept, (b) their interests in the topic or concept or their general interests, and (c) their learner profiles.

Learners do not approach school or a particular unit of study as a blank slate. They come with experiences (or lack of experiences) that shape their readiness to learn and their interests in a particular subject area or a specific unit of study. Ignoring information about learners when teaching is very much like going bowling with the pins covered. There is no way of knowing which pins might be knocked down if the bowler cannot see the pins, just as there is no way of knowing how to approach teaching students if the teacher does not have information about the learners. The learning profile is an umbrella term encompassing four categories of influence on how children approach learning: gender, culture, intelligence preferences, and learning style (Tomlinson & Imbeau, 2010, pp. 17–18). The concept is fluid and relates to how children take in and process information. Learning profile is not synonymous with learning style.

The central position of the learner in instructional planning illustrates that all aspects of differentiated instruction are planned to facilitate learning among all students in the classroom. Educators frequently say, "It is all about the kids." Differentiation is all about the learners—it is all about kids learning.

Learner Outcomes

Learner outcomes are at the core of the EDM. Planning is always the first step to take in differentiating. Without clear goals or learner outcomes, it would be impossible to defend different learning experiences for different children. Preassessment garners meaning when children are assessed for what they know, understand, and can do in relation to the learner outcomes.

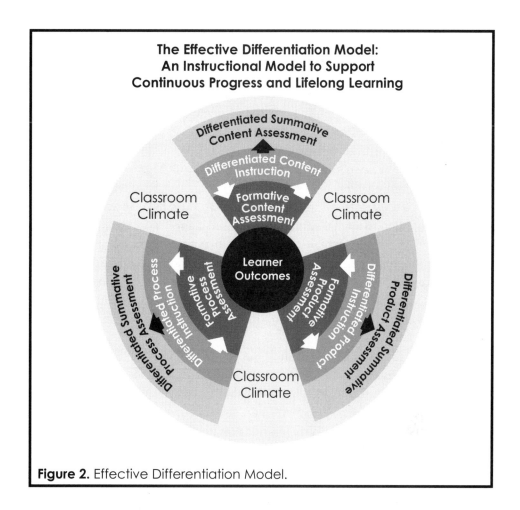

Figure 2. Effective Differentiation Model.

Content, Process, Product, and Assessment

Differentiation occurs in various instructional components. They include content, process, and product, which are illustrated on the three pie-shaped areas on the model. It is possible to differentiate in only one component or in two or more of them. Teachers differentiate content, process, or product, and then can extend differentiation with the assessment. Content, process, product, and assessment are components of learning experiences, and they can be matched to learners for effective differentiation.

Content relates to what is taught. It includes the concepts and information the teachers want students to learn, as well as the skills that they want them to master. Content falls along a continuum from basic to complex. Almost any concept that is taught in an elementary classroom also can be taught in a graduate course, so there is no limit to the depth at which students can engage in learning if preassessments indicate learners are ready for the advanced content. Standards often provide the content for classrooms, and the Common Core State Standards for English Language Arts and the Common Core State Standards for Mathematics define the content in most states.

Process describes the cognitive skills that are to be developed as learning experiences are implemented. In high-level learning experiences, learners will engage their minds in addition to their hands; hands-on learning lacks meaning unless it is linked with minds-on learning. Cognitive skills also come along a continuum from basic to complex. Thinking skills rank high as an emphasis in 21st-century learning.

Products are ways that children show what they have learned. Ways to demonstrate learning are not limited to pen-and-paper tests; they also include posters, models, videos, exhibitions, and performances (among others), all of which are included when we use the term *product* in this book. Products can be categorized in various ways, such as kinesthetic, oral, technological, visual, and written (Roberts & Inman, 2009b, pp. 8–9). Authentic products provide motivation for learners. Products provide a real tie to the world of work, as professionals use products.

Formative assessment establishes the starting point for learning experiences that differentiate content, process, and/or product. Later the assessment must be differentiated to match the areas that have been differentiated in the learning experiences. The assessment must provide opportunities for the learners to demonstrate what they have learned and may be differentiated in varying tiers with the Developing and Assessing Products Tool (DAP Tool; see Chapter 4) or with different rubrics that learners can follow in developing products and teachers can use in assessing those products.

Elementary teachers differentiate the content, process, and products as they plan learning experiences and match them to children's levels of readiness, interests, and learning profiles. As students engage in varied learning experiences, there is a need to differentiate the assessment as well. All children will make continuous progress and be on their way to becoming lifelong learners only when differentiation characterizes a classroom.

Differentiated learning experiences respond to the learners and match the components of learning—content, process, and products—to the learners. Effective differentiated learning experiences relate closely to learners and to the learning outcomes. Differentiation is intentional, and it is anchored in the goals of continuous progress and lifelong learning. These two goals set the stage for differentiated learning while information about the learners provide the motivation for differentiating.

Classroom Climate

Establishing a positive classroom climate is a requirement in a differentiated classroom, as differentiation will not work in classrooms that do not support different children learning at different levels and in different ways. In the EDM, the classroom climate provides the background to support differentiation. It provides the environment that puts learning front and center for all children. The teacher in a differentiated classroom must create an environment that supports diversity; promotes excellence, high expectations, and risk taking; and uses assessment to match instruction to levels of readiness, interests, and learning profiles. Such a classroom establishes the right environment for differentiation. Learners work separately; in pairs, triads, and small groups; and in a whole-group setting. In each of those configurations, children are a community of learners. The key consideration is for all children to learn on an ongoing basis and to become both independent learners and productive members of a group.

Goals for Differentiation

The EDM highlights the immediate and long-term goals of schooling in its subtitle: An Instructional Model to Support Continuous Progress and Lifelong Learning. Those goals shape all planning for the classroom, as children are not identical. Teachers who differentiate believe it is necessary so that all learners make continuous progress and are on the way to being lifelong learners.

Concluding Comments

There are basic components that must be included in effective differentiation. Teachers must always start their planning with learner outcomes, which are usually the standards. They must know that they can differentiate content, process, and/or products to ensure that learning experiences allow children to make continuous progress by extending their learning. Of course, differentiated learning experiences must be accompanied with assessments—preassessment (a type of formative assessment) to determine the starting place, formative assessment to shape learning experiences, and summative assessment to measure progress. All differentiated learning experiences are set against a classroom climate that supports respect, high expectations, and risk taking. The EDM offers a visual to keep front and center when thinking about, planning for, and implementing differentiated learning experiences.

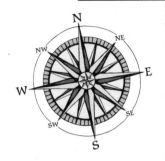

Survival Tips

- If the Effective Differentiation Model resonates with you, share it with a colleague or colleagues. Doing so does two things: It confirms that you understand the connections between the components of the model, and it lets others know of your interest in working to differentiate for children in your classroom and school.

- Discuss with an educator who is also interested in differentiation why each dimension of the Effective Differentiation Model is essential for differentiating successfully.

Survival Toolkit

- Differentiation Central (http://differentiationcentral.com): This site offers a plethora of resources about differentiation so that users can "Reach Every Learner Every Day Through Differentiated Instruction."

3 Content and Process Matter

[There are] one-story intellects, two-story intellects, and three-story intellects with skylights. All fact collectors, who have no aim beyond their facts, are one-story men. Two-story men compare, reason, generalize, using the labor of the fact collectors as their own. Three-story men idealize, imagine, predict; their best illumination comes from above, through the skylight.

—Oliver Wendell Holmes, Sr.

Key Question

- How do content and process combine to be prime ways to differentiate instruction?

Standards provide the starting place in the selection of appropriate content and cognitive goals or processes in most classrooms. The Common Core State Standards (National Governors Association Center for Best Practices & Council of Chief State School Officers, 2010a, 2010b) guide curriculum development in most states with standards in mathematics and language arts currently available. Standards in science also have been drafted, and revisions are currently being made. The American Association of School Librarians (2007) has standards for 21st-century learners. The 2010 NAGC Pre-K–Grade 12

Gifted Education Programming Standards were developed with student outcomes as the focus, and they provide guidance on many aspects of teaching and learning, including differentiation. These standards provide the research to back up recommended practices.

Standards specify content and also address process. Because all learning experiences include content and process, these two aspects of curriculum development are discussed in this one chapter. Both content and process provide opportunities for differentiating learning experiences. In the Effective Differentiation Model (see Chapter 2), content and process are two of the three main areas in which teachers differentiate. The third area to differentiate is student products (see Chapter 4). Then, learning experiences focused on differentiating content, process, and/or product must be accompanied by differentiated assessment.

Content

The starting place for designing differentiated learning experiences is the content. As discussed in Chapter 2, content is what teachers want students to know, understand, and be able to do. Content should not be selected because it is the teacher's favorite unit or because it was taught last year and thus readily available. The key consideration in selecting content is that it must be worth knowing. It must be selected for a solid, defensible instructional purpose.

Content can be basic, complex, or somewhere in between. Some students may be ready to learn basic information about the concept/content while others demonstrate on a preassessment that they are ready for a study of the concept that is more complex. A strategy to make the content more complex is to address issues and problems related to the concept. For example, some students may be ready to learn the basic information about the water cycle. Other children have the facts about the water cycle down pat, and they are ready to look at issues and problems related to water as a natural resource that must be preserved. All children are studying water but at different levels.

The National Association for Gifted Children (NAGC) standards address the need for content to be complex and challenging. For example, Standard 3.1.4 states, "Educators design differentiated curricula that incorporate advanced, conceptually challenging, in-depth, distinctive, and complex content for students with gifts and talents" (NAGC, 2010).

Deeper Learning

Deeper learning is "the process through which an individual becomes capable of taking what was learned in one situation and applying it to new situations (i.e., transfer)" (National Research Council, 2012, p. 4). The National Research Council (2012) recommended several instructional strategies, including:

- using multiple and varied representations of concepts and tasks;
- encouraging elaboration, questioning, and explanation;
- engaging learners in challenging tasks;
- teaching with examples and cases;
- priming student motivation by connecting topics; and
- using formative assessment. (pp. 6–7)

When planning for their content, teachers should remember that thinking more deeply is a means to creating an independent learner—a lifelong learner.

Primary Sources and Multiple Texts

Primary documents offer rich resources for students. Using primary resources is a great way to encourage the development of skills required for critical analysis of texts. Going back to the original source is encouraged as a strategy for literary analysis.

Use of multiple resources provides opportunities for children to read about the concept or topic at their reading levels. The emphasis on literacy makes it imperative that books and other written resources, both in print and online, are readily available for the readers in any grade level. The fact that readers in any elementary classroom may span 3–7 grades highlights that one set of books cannot be appropriately challenging for all of them. It is important not to limit available texts as long as the reader comprehends the reading material, but all resources must be high in quality.

In order to address the reading levels of all students in a class, teachers need to be aware of the lexile levels of materials being offered to students. Resources are available to help teachers know the lexile levels of resources in order to have appropriately challenging materials for all children, including those who read below grade level, at grade level, or above (or way above) grade level. The Lexile Framework for Reading (http://lexile.com/fab) is a ready resource for assessing the lexile level.

Rigor as a Relative Concept

Content needs to be rigorous for all learners. To be rigorous for all learners at one grade level means that the teacher must differentiate the learning experiences. Curriculum keeps the same focus for all children, but learning experiences must be matched to readiness. For example, reading level is one match that must be made if all children are to be appropriately challenged in study. Other examples include matching learning experiences to children's readiness to learn about fractions, insects, and the state in which the children live. Basic information is an appropriate match for children who don't yet have that knowledge, but children who demonstrate on a preassessment or in other ways that they know the basic information need learning experiences that will enhance their learning on the concepts. Rigor is certainly a relative concept, as what is rigorous for one third grader will not be rigorous at all for another one.

Process

Process sets the cognitive levels students use to learn the content. The same content can be matched to students' levels of readiness by ratcheting up the cognitive challenge, requiring learners to stretch and think about the content in ways they have not previously encountered. Thinking at high levels is a very important component of learning. Process involves preparing thinkers and independent learners—ones who can think critically and creatively, problem solve, and be independent investigators.

21st-Century Skills

Various individuals and groups have attempted to describe what constitutes 21st-century skills. Despite the differences they've found, all of the versions of 21st-century skills highlight processes that are essential for lifelong learners, including high-level thinking, creative thinking, and critical thinking. For example, the Partnership for 21st Century Skills (2011) listed four essential skills: critical thinking and problem solving, communication, collaboration, and creativity. In addition, Wagner (2008) described seven survival skills needed for the future: critical thinking and problem solving, collaboration across networks and leading by influence, agility and adaptability, initiative and entrepreneurialism, effective oral and written communication, accessing and analyzing information, and curiosity and imagination. Darling-Hammond (as cited in Umphrey, 2010) also listed 21st-century skills needed by students to be successful as adults, including:

> critical thinking and problem solving and the ability to identify and synthesize and analyze information, to develop resources and use them in novel situations, to work collaboratively with others, to frame a problem, to reflect on one's own learning, and to continue to improve the products and performances that one is engaged in without always having to rely on someone else to manage the work. The final dimension is the ability to learn to learn: to be able to learn new things on one's own, to be self-guided and independent in the learning process. (p. 18)

The Revised Bloom's Taxonomy

Bloom's (1956) Taxonomy of Cognitive Objectives is well known among educators, and the taxonomy provides a way to look at the level of thinking skills being addressed by a question or a learning experience. The revised taxonomy (Anderson et al., 2001) changed the levels to verbs and reversed the processes at the top two levels. From the top to the bottom, the levels in the revised taxonomy are create, evaluate, analyze, apply, understand, and remember. Filtering lessons through Bloom's taxonomy is a powerful way of ensuring high-level thinking and differentiation through process.

Thinking Like Mathematicians, Scientists, Writers, and Historians

The Common Core State Standards emphasize the importance of thinking as professionals such as mathematicians, scientists, writers, and historians do. That means that children are not merely memorizing facts, formulas, and information, but rather asking questions, pursuing their responses, and solving problems that are loosely structured. They are studying concepts to learn as much about them as they can. They are becoming engaged in their own learning, which means they are on their way to becoming lifelong learners.

Looking at a Topic or Concept From Multiple Perspectives

Important problems in society are not limited to one solution but rather have multiple perspectives that can be explored. Analyzing multiple perspectives enhances the complexity of the processing. If major problems in the world had only one possible solution, they would not continue to be problems. Children need to explore possibilities and then communicate the potential solution or perspective to others. It is very likely that children will draw upon what they are learning in different content areas as they probe questions and look for solutions to problems. This type of thinking does not happen when children produce a report that describes what they found out about a topic or when they answer low-level questions about the topic.

Creative Thinking and Problem Solving

The three lists of 21st-century skills presented in this chapter detail creativity, curiosity and imagination, and developing new products and ideas as featured skills. Creativity must be valued by teachers and actively promoted in a classroom if children are to be encouraged to think creatively. The Developing and Assessing Products Tool includes creativity as one of four components (see Chapter 4). Children are to think creatively about the content of a product as well as the presentation of the product itself. That is one way to hold creativity as important in a classroom on an ongoing basis, not just every now and then.

Concluding Comments

Teachers must differentiate content, process, and/or products to ensure that learning experiences allow children to make continuous progress. This chapter has focused on content and process, and the next chapter will examine how teachers can differentiate products to address the readiness, interests, and learning profiles of their students.

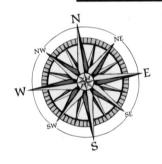

Survival Tips

- Remember that differentiated learning experiences have all children studying the same content or topic but at different levels, so all children are involved in the discussion. Everyone contributes and learns from each other, yet each student is learning what he is ready to learn.

- Students who see success in school as giving right answers are not prepared to be successful in postsecondary opportunities and are not on the way to becoming lifelong learners.

- Differentiating content and process in learning experiences is important in order to provide the appropriate level of challenge to all of your students.

- When you differentiate regularly, you will begin to see yourself as a talent developer.

Survival Toolkit

- Eberle, B., & Stanish, B. (1996). *CPS for kids*. Waco, TX: Prufrock Press. This book provides strategies for helping children learn to be creative problem solvers.

- Karnes, F. A., & Stephens, K. R. (2013). *The ultimate guide to Internet resources for teachers of gifted students*. Waco, TX: Prufrock Press. This book guides teachers in the use of Internet resources and highlights online resources that extend learning for children.

- Treffinger, D. J. (2000). *Practice problems for Creative Problem Solving* (3rd ed.). Waco, TX: Prufrock Press. This book helps teachers engage students in Creative Problem Solving.

- 7 Skills Students Need for Their Future (http://www.youtube.com/watch?v=NS2PqTTxFFc): This YouTube video features Tony Wagner describing his seven skills students need to know for their future success.

- American Association of School Librarians Standards for the 21st Century Learner (http://www.ala.org/aasl/sites/ala.org.aasl/files/content/guidelinesandstandards/learningstandards/AASL_Learning_Standards_2007.pdf): This page allows teachers to download a copy of the American Association of School Librarians standards for 21st-century learners.

- Common Core State Standards Initiative (http://www.corestandards.org): The Common Core State Standards' website has a text complexity section where text exemplars are organized into text complexity bands for different grade levels. They are to be used to show an on-grade-level example of text complexity.

- The Lexile Framework for Reading (http://lexile.com/fab/): Consider Lexile levels (reading levels) and text complexity when appropriately challenging students. Lexile's website has a feature that produces texts according to Lexile level and interests—a wonderful tool to use when the educator differentiates complexity.

- A Treasury of Primary Documents (http://www.constitution.org/primarysources/primarysources.html): This is a great source to retrieve primary documents from American history to use with learners.

4 Products: Demonstrations of Learning

Through the creation of products, students are able to move beyond mere acquisition of knowledge to application, analysis, and synthesis of content, concepts, and ideas.

—Kristen R. Stephens and Frances A. Karnes

Key Questions

- How can students demonstrate what they have learned?
- How can products be used as a way to differentiate learning experiences?

As the previous chapter described, teachers can differentiate instruction through their content—what they want students to know, understand, and be able to do—and their process—the cognitive levels students use to learn the content. Educators can also differentiate the product—how students show what they've learned. Products are vehicles for communicating information and/or demonstrating skills for specific purposes to authentic audiences. Allowing appropriate choice in products can be very motivating to students; in fact, providing an array of learning options for students has been shown to be a component of ideal learning environments (Jensen, 1998). Providing choice within limits (Fay & Funk, 1995) is the key to product differentiation.

When the product is the content, such as an English teacher instructing eighth graders on the elements of an argumentative essay (i.e., Common Core English Language Arts Standard W.8.1), then, of course, differentiation of product is not appropriate. Educators could have students choose the content to argue, the audience to address, the evidence to support, and so forth, but the end product is nonnegotiable—an argumentative essay. Choice of product is most apropos when teachers are more focused on content or process than the product. For example, a science teacher wants to assess a student's understanding of mitosis. It doesn't matter to her if the student presents that understanding through an illustrated diagram, a model, or an essay. The concept outranks the product. Of course, it is critical that the content be accurate and logically presented and show a depth of understanding, but it is also critical that the product itself is of high quality—more on that a bit later.

Why is it important to use a variety of products in instruction and assessment? Some of the most compelling reasons follow (Roberts & Inman, 2009a):

- Products are engaging.
- Products are motivating.
- Products have "real-world" connections.
- Well-developed products require high-level thinking and problem-solving skills.
- Products provide a practical way for teachers to match learning experiences to students' preferred ways of learning.
- Products allow for and encourage self-expression and creativity.
- Products foster pride in one's work.
- Products develop lifelong learners. (pp. 2–3)

Product development, when used appropriately in the classroom, taps into the four Cs of 21st-century learning skills: critical thinking and problem solving, communication, collaboration, and creativity and innovation (Partnership for 21st Century Skills, 2009). Critical and creative thinking regarding both content and product are required for high-level products. Products are vehicles of communication—an architect constructs a model to communicate his ideas for a new hospital, the latest Hollywood blockbuster-hopeful plasters movie posters across the nation hoping to entice moviegoers, and a nonprofit creates a user-friendly, informative, and attractive web page to explain its purpose and mission to possible supporters. Products are all about the communication of ideas! Students can also develop collaboration skills when they work in pairs or small groups to create products.

Please realize that the product discussed in this chapter is not the character sketch hastily scrawled on lined paper, the poem made up on the bus ride to school, or the ad-libbed monologue given in class by the child who forgot the assignment. It is also not the beautifully animated PowerPoint that blends video and graphics masterfully yet contains unimportant or incorrect content. Nor is it the "literature-based arts and crafts" (Calkins, Montgomery, & Santman, 1998, p. 51) that lack substance, critical thinking, and creativity—something that is hands-on only, not minds-on, too. Rather, this product "is a rich culminating assessment that calls on students to apply and extend what they have learned over a period of time" (Tomlinson & Imbeau, 2010, p. 15). Therefore, products must be tied to curricular objectives; they are neither fillers for when time is miscalculated, nor are they fluff tasks tacked onto a unit.

Points to Consider

Before educators create product lists, assignments, and rubrics, there are a few questions to answer:

- *Purpose*: What is the purpose of the product? Will it be a summative assessment? A project that accompanies a unit? An anchor project? An independent study for someone who has mastered the material?
- *Time*: How long will the products take to complete? Do the selected products require similar completion time? Is time needed in class for students to work?
- *Resources*: Do your students have the necessary resources to complete the product? Is it possible to furnish the resources and supplies? How will that happen? How and where will the supplies be stored? Do technology labs need to be scheduled?
- *Experience*: Does the educator have experience in creating the products selected? What experience do the students have with creating specific products? Does the product itself need to be taught? Should examples be shown? Has the product criteria been explained?
- *Assessment*: How will the products be graded? Have rubrics been created? Will online sites be used to create the rubric? Will students create their own? Will another source be used to create the rubric? How will the educator decide what makes an excellent product? How can the teacher assess that the product is authentic and that it demonstrates understanding of the intended concepts?

Although the educator may not need definitive answers to every single question, the point is that a product list must be conscientiously constructed. It can't be based on whimsy. It can't contain products students have no idea how to create. It can't list products that take too much time or require unattainable resources. It certainly can't offer products that the teacher does not feel comfortable with assessing at high standards. As the educational professional, the teacher decides what is appropriate and why it is appropriate. This is true of any product list. However, if the goal is to differentiate via products, the educator must think about a few more things before he creates that list.

Differentiating With Products

Often, well-meaning educators mistakenly believe that handing a student a list of a half-dozen product choices is differentiating. It isn't. Granted, such a list may be appealing and motivating to students, but product differentiation is an intentional match between product choices and the individual students. It is an educational strategy designed to encourage continuous progress for students. For example, a teacher differentiating based on learning preferences may create one list of kinesthetic products, one of visual products, one with written options, and so on. Then, when the visual learners have the choice of multiple visual products to demonstrate their understanding of content, differentiation happens. "Product development helps to individualize learning experiences so students can express themselves in ways that are most relevant to their own style of information processing" (Stephens & Karnes, 2009, p. 162).

Before educators can differentiate with products, they must preassess. This could be a multiple intelligences inventory, a learning style inventory, an interest inventory, a readiness measure to determine who's ready to work on what level, or something like *My Way . . . An Expression Style Inventory* (Kettle, Renzulli, & Rizza, 1998) that uses students' responses to match students to preferred product options. Educators (Armstrong, 2000; Heacox, 2002; Teele, 1996) have created inventories based on Gardner's (1983) multiple intelligences theory. A myriad of learning style or learning preference inventories abound, from Dunn and Dunn's (2010) online learning styles models to Silver, Strong, and Perini's (2000) process-oriented learning styles model. The approach used is secondary to the reason to use it—determining individual student preferences for learning so that appropriate product choice is possible. Product preference and interest inventories prove useful in differentiating products as well. Figure 3 is a preassessment for a lesson focusing on English Language Arts Reading Literature Standard 3.3: "Describe characters in a story (e.g., their traits, motivations, or feelings) and explain how their actions contribute to the sequence of events" (National Governors Association Center for Best Practices & Council of Chief State School Officers, 2010a). The product choices are based on learning preferences with kinesthetic ones listed in the first line, oral in the second, then technological, then visual, and finally written products. Note the question regarding grouping. Allowing students a choice in whether they work alone or with a group is a simple differentiation strategy. This preassessment helps the teacher narrow product choices according to interest and/or experience, discover which products need to be taught, and form groups if needed. This 5-minute

---

Exploration of Character Preassessment

As part of the short story unit, we will be analyzing characters—their personalities, their reasons for acting they way they do, their feelings, and so on. We will also examine how their thoughts and actions contribute to the story itself. You will have a choice in how you present your analysis. Please answer the questions below so that I can better create the assignment to meet your needs.

1. Circle those products listed below that you have created before.
2. Put a star beside those products that interest you.
3. Put a check beside those products that interest you that you have not created before.

sculpture	mask	model	skit
debate	interview	monologue	oral presentation
blog	movie	podcast	PowerPoint presentation
cartoon	collage	pamphlet	newspaper article
poster	diary	letter	written interview

4. Would you prefer to
    work alone?
    work with a partner(s)?

Figure 3. Exploration of character preassessment.

---

preassessment can make all the difference in student motivation and learning throughout the unit. Remember that the more information a teacher has about students, the better she is able to differentiate.

Once the teacher has decided how he will use products to differentiate—whether that's based on needs, interests, abilities, or learning preferences—it's time to develop the product list. Although certainly not exhaustive, the product list in Figure 4 suggests products categorized according to learning preference (Roberts & Inman, 2009b). When students are able to be instructed and assessed in a manner matching their learning profiles, they tend to perform better (Grigorenko & Sternberg, 1997; Lovelace, 2005; Sternberg, 1997; Sternberg, Torff, & Grigorenko, 1998). Educators may want to offer only a couple of options from each category. They need to think about time, resources, and their ability to assess the products, and make the list one that is both realistic and meaningful. Figure 5 contains products organized via multiple intelligences. When instruction includes an emphasis on multiple intelligences, students not only do better on tests (as a research study by Campbell and Campbell [1999] attested), but teachers and students have more positive attitudes about learning (as studies by Campbell and Campbell [1999] and Tomlinson, Callahan, and Lelli [1997] have purported). Note that several products overlap because just

Product List: Learning Preferences				
Kinesthetic	**Oral**	**Technological**	**Visual**	**Written**
dance	debate	blog	book jacket	critique
diorama	interview	documentary	brochure	essay
demonstration	monologue	Facebook page	cartoon	journal
experiment	presentation	PowerPoint presentation	collage	lyrics
model	radio ad	Prezi	drawing	newspaper article
sculpture	role-play	Twitter feed	museum display	poem
simulation	song	video	painting	short story
skit	speech	web page	poster	technical report

Figure 4. Product list: Learning preferences.

as a single product may address multiple learning preferences, a single product can also pertain to more than one multiple intelligence.

Providing product choice within certain educational parameters is an ideal way to meet students' needs through differentiation of product. Ideally, though, students need to investigate and create a wide variety of products. Therefore, educators need to be careful to encourage the student gifted in art to branch out to written or oral products and the intrapersonal learner to experiment with logical-mathematical or naturalist products. This "healthy risk-taking" (Stephens & Karnes, 2009, p. 165) encourages them to make connections, develop self-confidence, and grow as learners. The point is to vary the differentiation approach—differentiate content, process, and product at various times throughout the school year. Teachers shouldn't just differentiate product according to multiple intelligences every time.

Product differentiation can be very beneficial for students who are twice-exceptional or multiexceptional, in that not only are they identified as gifted and talented in one or more areas, but they are also identified as having a learning difficulty, autism spectrum disorder, Attention Deficit/Hyperactivity Disorder, or physical impairment. When choice is allowed, students can focus on their strengths (Karnes & Stephens, 2009; Trail, 2012). To ask a student with dysgraphia for a written product would probably result in a frustrated student with a poor product. That student should develop a product that utilizes her strengths (Trail, 2012).

Product List: Multiple Intelligences

Visual-Spatial	Bodily-Kinesthetic	Logical-Mathematical	Naturalist	Musical-Rhythmic	Verbal-Linguistic	Interpersonal	Intrapersonal
drawing	charades	chart	classification system	poem	critique	advertisement	collage
flow chart	dance	computer program	diorama	performance	debate	Facebook page	journal
graph	experiment	experiment	documentary	podcast	essay	interview	letter
model	game	graph	exhibit	radio play	interview	journal	memoir
movie	model	graphic organizer	experiment	rap	journal	letter	monologue
photo essay	performance	model	journal	score	poem	role-play	opinion piece/ editorial
poster	role-play	technical report	log	song	short story	survey	scrapbook
sculpture	skit	word problem	museum display	soundtrack	speech	Twitter feed	self-portrait

Figure 5. Product list: Multiple Intelligences.

Product Assessment

For students to develop 21st-century skills such as problem solving and critical and creative thinking through product development, then products must be assessed at high standards. Students (and educators) must understand the essential criteria in individual products and what constitutes excellence. Learners need rubrics or scoring guides that encourage them to take on the next level of challenge. They must acknowledge the vital role that products play in the real world so that they connect their learning to their future.

A rubric should be both a guide for student development of the product and one for teacher assessment of the product. It should clearly describe the critical components of the product itself using non-content-specific vocabulary (Karnes & Stephens, 2009; Roberts & Inman, 2009b; Stanley, 2012)—and these components should be what professionals in the field consider them to be. The rubric also needs to assess content accuracy, coherence, and complexity; after all, learning content is the reason for product creation. Creativity—that personal insight the student brings to both the content and the product—should also be addressed (Carr, 2009; Roberts & Inman, 2009a). Ideally it includes a metacognitive component where the student reflects about his learning (Marzano, Pickering, & McTighe, 1993; Roberts & Inman, 2009a). Remember that the vocabulary should not be content-related, so that the rubric can be used across content and concept areas.

In addition to the categories of assessment, a rubric needs a clear grading scale, one that removes the learning ceiling: "All children and youth benefit when the learning ceiling is removed, as they need opportunities to become the best learners they can be" (Roberts & Roberts, 2009, p. 187). Too often, high-ability children and children who have gifts and talents are able to produce strong work with little effort. Additionally, they tend to expect the highest ranking or grade and may be disappointed with less than that. Therefore, in order to challenge students and nurture excellence, a grading scale without a ceiling is critical (Roberts & Inman, 2009a). For example, Roberts and Inman's Developing and Assessing Products Tool (DAP Tool; 2009a) has seven levels including two that go beyond the proficient expectation: advanced and professional. They argue that an educator may never once mark that professional level throughout her entire career, but students need to know that there is room for improvement even with excellent products; they also need to know that professionals strive for excellence. (Please note Roberts and Inman also believe that students' grades should not be penalized with such a scale; an A may equate to an advanced-level assessment, not the professional level.) A grading scale should be clearly defined so that the meaning of each ranking is clear (Karnes & Stephens, 2009). A comments section or room for notes is also important in order to personalize and explain markings.

Roberts and Inman's (2009a) protocol, the DAP Tool, incorporates all of those elements (see Figure 6). Each DAP Tool, regardless of product, has the same four components: content (addressing accuracy, coherence, and complexity), presentation (those components that define the product), creativity, and reflection. In fact, three of the components are verbatim for every product (i.e., content, creativity, and reflection) to simplify the teaching and use of the rubric. Another innovation mentioned previously is the seven-level grading scale that removes the learning ceiling. Note, too, that there is a nonparticipation level for those who do nothing. Ideally the student would have the DAP Tool in front of him as he creates the product in order to be sure to include all of the critical components. The DAP Tool is just one resource that simplifies differentiation of products.

Many educators spend countless hours carefully developing rubrics for product development and assessment. That is definitely one strategy. But resources abound that can ease that burden. Multiple websites are devoted to rubric development and sharing. Not only do they have ready-made rubrics for easy use, but they also have customizable templates where the educator selects the type of rating scale, the critical components of the product, and the descriptors. A favorite is Kathy Schrock's Guide to Everything (http://schrockguide.net/assessment-and-rubrics.html), which houses dozens of rubrics plus links to rubric generators such as RubiStar (http://rubistar.4teachers.org). Educators should be careful when using already created rubrics—they shouldn't just print out a rubric without carefully examining it for high quality.

Print resources are also strong sources for product rubrics. For example, Carr (2009) described four basic types of products: those that students present, those that students construct, those that students draw or design, and those that students write. She created four rubrics, one for each type of product. These can be used across subject matter and across most grade levels. Each rubric contains critical elements of the product itself plus the concept of creativity. To make it even more user-friendly, she includes qualitative descriptors for her five-level grading scale and a conversion table to change scores to percentiles.

Curry and Samara's (1991) *Product Guide Kit* provides critical attributes of products categorized by visual, written, kinesthetic, and oral learning preferences. Easy to use, each product card guides the student as he creates the product and the educator as she assesses the product. A rubric can be easily made from the attributes. Easier still is the use of their StandardWriter Software (see http://www.curriculumproject.com/curry_samara_software_bundle_products.php) that creates customized rubrics electronically.

Another useful rubric resource is Karnes and Stephens' (2009) *The Ultimate Guide for Student Product Development and Evaluation*, now in its second edition. Categorized by learning style, each product in this book is not only thoroughly delineated by its critical attributes, but the product's page also has a

POSTER Tier 1—DAP TOOL

CONTENT	▪ Is the content correct and complete?	0 1 2 3 4 5 6
	▪ Has the content been thought about in a way that goes beyond a surface understanding?	0 1 2 3 4 5 6
	▪ Is the content put together in such a way that people understand it?	0 1 2 3 4 5 6
PRESENTATION		
TEXT	▪ Is the title easy to see, clear, and well placed? Do the labels clearly explain the graphics?	0 1 2 3 4 5 6
GRAPHICS	▪ Are the graphics (illustrations, photos) important and relevant to the topic?	0 1 2 3 4 5 6
LAYOUT	▪ Are the images carefully selected and emphasized? Is the labeling linked to the graphic? Is it pleasing to the eye? Is the spacing deliberate to draw attention to main parts of the poster?	0 1 2 3 4 5 6
CREATIVITY	▪ Is the content seen in a new way?	0 1 2 3 4 5 6
	▪ Is the presentation done in a new way?	0 1 2 3 4 5 6
REFLECTION	▪ What did you learn about the content as you completed this product?	0 1 2 3 4 5 6
	▪ What did you learn about yourself as a learner by creating this product?	0 1 2 3 4 5 6

Comments

_____

_____

Meaning of Performance Scale:
6—PROFESSIONAL LEVEL: level expected from a professional in the content area
5—ADVANCED LEVEL: level exceeds expectations of the standard
4—PROFICIENT LEVEL: level expected for meeting the standard
3—PROGRESSING LEVEL: level demonstrates movement toward the standard
2—NOVICE LEVEL: level demonstrates initial awareness and knowledge of standard
1—NONPERFORMING LEVEL: level indicates no effort made to meet standard
0—NONPARTICIPATING LEVEL: level indicates nothing turned in

Figure 6. DAP Tool: Poster. From *Assessing Differentiated Student Products* (p. 141) by J. L. Roberts and T. F. Inman, 2009, Waco, TX: Prufrock Press. Copyright 2009 Prufrock Press. Reprinted with permission.

wealth of information about it for the educator and the student to use: definitions, types of the product, quotes to inspire, community resources, words to know, helpful hints, and exemplary producers. The critical attributes can readily be transferred to a high-level rubric, one that students can use to create the product and one that teachers can use to assess it.

Coil (2004) provided Product Criteria Cards listing critical attributes for ease in product development and evaluation. Although not as detailed as some of the other products, they provide a jumpstart for students. Like Coil's Product Criteria Cards, student-friendly Product Pouches (Engine-Unity, 2005) list product criteria, but they also include a definition or description of the product itself. Most of these resources list similar critical attributes for the same products, but it's always a good idea to make sure those attributes align with what experts in the field deem critical.

Marzano et al. (1993) explored performance assessment in relation to their Standards of Dimensions of Learning:

- Dimension 1: Positive attitudes and perceptions about learning.
- Dimension 2: Thinking needed to acquire and integrate new knowledge.
- Dimension 3: Thinking needed to extend and refine knowledge.
- Dimension 4: Thinking needed to use knowledge meaningfully.
- Dimension 5: Use of effective habits of mind. (p. 24)

The second half of their work contains exemplary rubrics based on standards for complex thinking, information processing, effective communication, collaboration/cooperation, and habits of mind like making effective plans and metacognition. Especially interesting are the rubrics for student self-assessment on these standards. These tie directly to the reflection component of the DAP Tool (Roberts & Inman, 2009a).

Emphasizing the importance of having different rubrics for each product, Stanley (2012) suggested empowering students to create their own. He argued that a student-made rubric "clearly shows students how work is being evaluated, clarifies what the expectations of the project are, allows students to set high expectations for themselves, and acts as a motivational tool for students" (p. 53). It does take time to teach students how to create rubrics because specific feedback is necessary, but the benefits seem worth it. Most challenging would be designing the critical attribute sections, but there are many resources (such as those listed above) that can guide the student. Note the common threads to the rubrics here: language reflective of the product—not the content—so rubrics can be used across subjects, the emphasis on creativity, and criteria descriptors that should help the student develop the product.

Differentiating Assessment

Most educators feel much more comfortable differentiating content, process, or product than they do differentiating assessment. Questions abound when it comes to differentiating assessment: How can I hold one student to one standard and another to a different standard? Is it fair? How do I know which student to hold to what standard? How do I explain it to the students? The parents? If the goal of education is continuous learning (and what parent or student does not want that?), then holding students to different standards—individually appropriate standards that challenge and encourage growth—is one way to meet that goal. The bottom line is that differentiation of assessment, when it comes to products, can be a very effective way to meet the needs of students.

POSTER Tier 2—DAP TOOL

CONTENT	• Content is accurate.	0 1 2 3 4 5 6
	• Content has depth and complexity of thought.	0 1 2 3 4 5 6
	• Content is organized.	0 1 2 3 4 5 6
PRESENTATION		
TEXT	• Title enhances the poster's purpose and is well placed. Text highlights most important concepts in topic.	0 1 2 3 4 5 6
GRAPHICS	• Graphics (illustrations, photos) add information and are appropriate for the topic.	0 1 2 3 4 5 6
LAYOUT	• Layout design clearly emphasizes graphics in an organized and attractive manner. Text is placed to clearly describe/explain all graphic images. Spacing is carefully planned with consideration of space not used.	0 1 2 3 4 5 6
CREATIVITY	• Individual insight is expressed in relation to the content.	0 1 2 3 4 5 6
	• Individual spark is expressed in relation to the presentation.	0 1 2 3 4 5 6
REFLECTION	• Reflection on the learning of the content through product development is apparent.	0 1 2 3 4 5 6
	• Reflection on what the student learned about self as a learner is apparent.	0 1 2 3 4 5 6

Comments

_____

_____

Meaning of Performance Scale:
6—PROFESSIONAL LEVEL: level expected from a professional in the content area
5—ADVANCED LEVEL: level exceeds expectations of the standard
4—PROFICIENT LEVEL: level expected for meeting the standard
3—PROGRESSING LEVEL: level demonstrates movement toward the standard
2—NOVICE LEVEL: level demonstrates initial awareness and knowledge of standard
1—NONPERFORMING LEVEL: level indicates no effort made to meet standard
0—NONPARTICIPATING LEVEL: level indicates nothing turned in

Figure 7. DAP Tool: Poster, Tier 2. From *Assessing Differentiated Student Products* (p. 142) by J. L. Roberts and T. F. Inman, 2009, Waco, TX: Prufrock Press. Copyright 2009 Prufrock Press. Reprinted with permission.

Differentiation of assessment is certainly not a new concept, especially in relation to children with special needs. What may be new, however, is differentiating assessment for gifted and talented children. Because some of these students may already know the material (Stanley, 2000), preassessment of content and process prove critical so that differentiation occurs. Differentiation of product becomes important as well, so students can continue to develop skills and strive for excellence.

One easy way to differentiate assessment is to have several versions of the same product rubric with one version more challenging or more sophisticated than the other, yet similar in appearance. For example, DAP Tools (Roberts & Inman, 2009a) have three tiers for each product. Look back at Figure 6, then notice in Figures 7 and 8 how each tier becomes more rigorous with greater expectations. Note the evolution of title under Presentation Text. Tier 1 asks "Is the title easy to see, clear, and well placed?" whereas Tier 2 reads "Title enhances the

POSTER Tier 3—DAP TOOL

CONTENT			
	• Content is accurate and thorough in detail.		0 1 2 3 4 5 6
	• Product shows complex understanding and manipulation of content.		0 1 2 3 4 5 6
	• Product shows deep probing of content.		0 1 2 3 4 5 6
	• Organization is best suited to the product.		0 1 2 3 4 5 6
PRESENTATION			
	TEXT	• Title, clearly reflecting purpose, is strategically placed. Text highlights most important concepts in clear, concise manner.	0 1 2 3 4 5 6
	GRAPHICS	• Graphics (illustrations, photos) enhance meaning and are best suited for the purpose.	0 1 2 3 4 5 6
	LAYOUT	• Successful composition of graphic images and design concepts communicates the purpose. Text is strategically placed to enhance the message of the poster. Negative space is used to highlight key points.	0 1 2 3 4 5 6
CREATIVITY	• Individual insight is originally expressed in relation to the content.		0 1 2 3 4 5 6
	• Individual spark is originally expressed in relation to the presentation.		0 1 2 3 4 5 6
REFLECTION	• Insightful reflection on the learning of the content through product development is expressed.		0 1 2 3 4 5 6
	• Insightful reflection on what the student learned about self as a learner is expressed.		0 1 2 3 4 5 6

Comments

_____

_____

Meaning of Performance Scale:
6—PROFESSIONAL LEVEL: level expected from a professional in the content area
5—ADVANCED LEVEL: level exceeds expectations of the standard
4—PROFICIENT LEVEL: level expected for meeting the standard
3—PROGRESSING LEVEL: level demonstrates movement toward the standard
2—NOVICE LEVEL: level demonstrates initial awareness and knowledge of standard
1—NONPERFORMING LEVEL: level indicates no effort made to meet standard
0—NONPARTICIPATING LEVEL: level indicates nothing turned in

Figure 8. DAP Tool: Poster, Tier 3. From *Assessing Differentiated Student Products* (p. 143) by J. L. Roberts and T. F. Inman, 2009, Waco, TX: Prufrock Press. Copyright 2009 Prufrock Press. Reprinted with permission.

poster's purpose and is well placed," while Tier 3 is even more stringent: "Title, clearly reflecting purpose, is strategically placed." A student who has never created a poster may need Tier 1 while an artistically gifted young person may need Tier 3. The matching of rubric to student must be based on preassessment.

Concluding Comments

Offering appropriate choices of authentic products can be a powerful avenue for differentiation and a strong motivator for students.

Choice serves as a natural motivator and allows students to feel empowered in their learning because they have some say in what and how they learn. The specific areas in which students have choice are up to the teacher, but by providing choice, the teacher also provides greater passion for learning. (Stanley, 2012, p. 10)

Differentiation occurs when teachers match the list of product choices to the learner, and that match can be based on concepts such as learning profiles, multiple intelligences, or interests. Educators must hold students to high standards in product development. Rubrics that describe critical product components can serve both as a guide for the students as they create the product and as assessment tool when teachers evaluate the learning as demonstrated in that product.

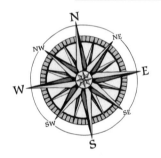

Survival Tips

- Be intentional about the product lists. Ask yourself, "Why does this child get this particular list of products to demonstrate learning about this particular concept or content?" Remember that handing students lists of products isn't necessarily differentiating.

- Use general rubrics designed for a certain product. A poster rubric can be used with a second-grade class learning about communities or a high school French class conjugating verbs.

- Utilize already-created rubrics or product criteria guides, but only if they are of high quality.

- Warehouse the general rubrics to make it easy to allow students even more choice.

- Distribute the rubric along with the assignment so that students are cognizant of the requirements and expectations before getting started.

- Collect examples of products to help students understand the various levels of assessment. It helps them understand excellence when they see it.

- Take the ceiling off of the grading scale to encourage excellence in all students, including those who are gifted and talented and of high ability. However, don't expect students to reach that professional or highest level, and don't penalize their grades by making the professional level the only way to earn an A.

- Have students reflect on their learning and on the development of the product: What did they learn about the content by creating this product? What did they learn about themselves as learners by creating this product?

- Base differentiating decisions on preassessments, whether that be differentiation of the product itself or of the assessment of the product.

Survival Toolkit

- Curry, J., & Samara, J. (1991). *Product guide kit.* Austin, TX: Curriculum Project. Based on learning styles, this kit outlines critical components of products as well as descriptors of those attributes.

- Engine-Uity. (2005). *Product pouch 2.* Phoeniz, AZ: Author. This teacher-created resource defines and describes a multitude of products in a very student-friendly way.

- Karnes, F. A., & Stephens, K. R. (2009). *The ultimate guide for student product development and evaluation* (2nd ed.). Waco, TX: Prufrock Press. From definition of the product to exemplary producers to critical components, this resource provides quality information that will assist the child in developing the product and the educator in assessing it.

- Roberts, J. L., & Inman, T. F. (2009). *Assessing differentiated student products: A protocol for development and evaluation.* Waco, TX: Prufrock Press. The dozens of DAP Tools contained in this resource make product differentiation and assessment doable.

- Stephens, K. R., & Karnes, F. A. (2009). Product development for gifted students. In F. A. Karnes & S. M. Bean (Eds.), *Methods and materials for teaching the gifted* (3rd ed., pp. 157–186). Waco, TX: Prufrock Press. Based on research, this chapter provides crucial information and best practices regarding products.

- Kathy Shrock's Guide to Everything: Assessment and Rubrics (http://www.schrockguide.net/assessment-and-rubrics.html): From subject-specific rubrics, to multimedia rubrics and collaboration rubrics, to rubric generators (and more!), this website is a gold mine of resources.

5 Culture: Creating a Classroom Climate to Support Differentiation

I've come to a frightening conclusion that I am the decisive element in the classroom. It's my personal approach that creates the climate. It's my daily mood that makes the weather. As a teacher, I possess a tremendous power to make a child's life miserable or joyous. I can be a tool of torture or an instrument of inspiration. I can humiliate or heal. In all situations, it is my response that decides whether a crisis will be escalated or de-escalated and a child humanized or dehumanized.

—Haim G. Ginott

Key Question

- How do teachers create and support a culture of differentiation in their classrooms?

Although the word *frightening* stirs images of movie villains and ghostly specters, it correctly connotes the intense responsibility educators have for the culture of their classroom. Tragically, words like *miserable, tool of torture, humiliate,* and *dehumanized* can be associated with the educational experience for some children. Educators do not always put the appropriate emphasis on the learning environment they establish. As Ginott stressed in this chapter's opening quote, the educator is indeed the decisive element in the classroom. This is especially true in the differentiated classroom. As Tomlinson and Imbeau (2010) argued,

> It is certainly the case that teachers who lead effectively for differentiation operate from a clear sense that classrooms should model a world in which learning is rewarding and in which mutual respect, persistent effort, and shared responsibility make everyone stronger. (p. 26)

Educators must intentionally create and support a culture of differentiation in their classrooms.

Please note that this chapter is not about districtwide or even schoolwide differentiation; Hewitt and Weckstein's (2011) *Differentiation Is an Expectation: A School Leader's Guide to Building a Culture of Differentiation* can guide schools and districts beautifully through that process. This chapter, rather, addresses the differentiated classroom, the place where the teacher makes the most direct impact and, quite frankly, exerts the most control.

A Classroom Culture of Differentiation

Learning environment is "shaped by a teacher's beliefs, experiences, and actions" (Tomlinson & Imbeau, 2010, p. 19). So, in order to create and support a differentiated learning environment, educators must not only believe that a differentiated classroom is quintessential to learning, but their curriculum and pedagogy must reflect that belief. "A teacher who lives the differentiated lifestyle in the classroom views every aspect of his or her teaching, from the simplest to the most complex task, through a differentiated lens" (Westphal, 2011, p. 2).

How, then, does an educator create and support a classroom culture of differentiation? Educators must first celebrate diversity in their classrooms. They must also support challenge and risk taking while holding appropriately high expectations for their students. Their instruction is guided by continuous assessment. Procedures and routines provide the underpinning of instruction. These elements combine to ultimately provide a foundation for a strong community of learners and excellence in teaching. Each element, however, warrants further discussion and elaboration.

Support Diversity

Diversity is one of the National Council for Accreditation of Teacher Education's standards (NCATE, 2008, Standard 4), which ideally guide all teacher preparation institutions' curricula. In these standards, diversity is defined as "differences among groups of people and individuals based on ethnicity, race, socioeconomic status, gender, exceptionalities, language, religion, sexual orientation, and geographical areas" (p. 86). The category of exceptionalities, added in the revised standards, includes children who learn differently from the norm, whether that be a student with dyslexia or one identified as gifted in mathematics. Because preservice teachers typically take a diversity course, they at least understand, in theory, that students differ. NCATE also requires fieldwork hours in diverse settings for preservice teachers to gain insight and experience. Some teacher education students may have attended schools with diversity, so they can personally relate to the impact diversity has on the classroom environment and on learning. Regardless of the preparation, however, few teachers are really ready for the vast differences in their own students.

Not only do students vary from one another in regard to those areas listed above such as socioeconomic status and the language spoken in the home, but they also vary as learners. From multiple intelligences (Gardner, 1983) to learning styles (Dunn & Dunn, 2010; Silver et al., 2000), from specialized interests to readiness levels, students walk into the classroom with varying needs, interests, and abilities. Their learning profiles differ. According to Tomlinson and Imbeau (2010), learning profiles are shaped by learning style, intelligence preference, gender, and culture, as well as the interaction of these factors. In order for a climate of differentiation to thrive, these differences must be acknowledged and celebrated. A multitude of instruments exist (as described in the previous chapter) that help educators determine learning profiles.

Of course, educators must communicate the results of those assessments to both students and parents. It is important that students take ownership of their learning because metacognition (i.e., students thinking about their own thinking) plays a critical role in students' ability to learn and thrive (Gallagher, 2009). Costa and Kallick (2000) included metacognition as one of their 16 Habits of Mind that promote exceptional learning. The more students understand their learning styles and preferences, the better able they are to take charge of their learning. This knowledge and understanding empowers students and encourages them to take ownership of their education.

Perhaps the most important step in communicating to students that the classroom is a differentiated one and that diversity is celebrated and incorporated into learning starts with a discussion with students at the beginning of the school year. Tomlinson and Imbeau (2010) encouraged educators to ask the following questions:

1. Who are you as learners? (Are you all alike or are there important differences?)
2. Given the differences we see, how should I teach you?
3. If our classroom is going to work for all of us, what will it be like? (How will it need to function? What roles will each of us play?)

4. How can I learn more about your starting points, interests, and best ways of learning?
5. If we have a differentiated classroom, can it be fair? (What will "fair" mean in this room?)
6. What will success in this class mean? (How will I know if you're succeeding? How will you know?) (pp. 45–46)

Imagine the discussion that ensues! These simple questions invite students to play critical roles in their learning and in their success. They also establish the parameters for a differentiated classroom, one that celebrates diversity.

Celebrating diversity aligns nicely with the Council of Chief State School Officers' Interstate Teacher Assessment and Support Consortium (InTASC, 2011) *Model Core Teaching Standards: A Resource for State Dialogue.* This document outlined standards that

> articulate what effective teaching and learning looks like in a transformed public education system—one that empowers every learner to take ownership of their learning, that emphasizes the learning of content and application of knowledge and skill to real world problems, that values differences each learner brings to the learning experience, and that leverages rapidly changing learning environments by recognizing the possibilities they bring to maximize learning and engage learners. (p. 3)

Part of the essential knowledge for the teacher focuses on diversity: "The teacher understands that learners bring assets for learning based on their individual experiences, abilities, talents, prior learning, and peer and social group interactions, as well as language, culture, family, and community values" (InTASC, 2011, p. 11). This understanding nourishes the differentiated classroom.

Support Challenge, High Expectations, and Risk Taking

For the last decade, the United States has devoted billions of dollars to No Child Left Behind (Elementary and Secondary Education Act, 2002), essentially sending the message that proficiency is the goal for all American school children. For some children, this is right on target. To be proficient in certain content areas provides challenge and rigor; they learn and grow because the goal is appropriate for them. Others struggle tremendously, never really having a chance of reaching proficiency because the goal is unrealistic; school frustrates them. Others stagnate; those who have already reached proficiency before the school year starts or reach it very quickly languish in the classrooms because the goal is far too low. Data show that the achievement gap is indeed narrowing through NCLB; however, that gap is closing from the bottom up—the lowest achieving students are gaining ground while the highest achieving students remain static (Finn & Petrilla, 2008). In fact, Fordham Foundation's president Chester E. Finn, Jr., remarked:

> To its credit No Child Left Behind appears to be making progress toward its stated goal: narrowing achievement gaps from the bottom up. Let us celebrate the gains of our lowest achieving students. But in a time of fierce international competition, can we afford to let the strongest languish? As John Gardner once asked, "Can we be equal and excellent too?" Surely the answer must be yes. For America to maintain prosperity and strength on a shrinking, flattening planet, we need also to serve our ablest youngsters far better than we're doing today. (as cited in Kuhner, 2008, para. 2)

One way to be "equal and excellent" is to match content, process, and product to the child's readiness levels, interests, and learning profile. The goal should not be proficiency for all; the goal should be continuous progress for all. Therefore, the differentiated classroom has high expectations for all children, regardless of their readiness or ability levels. Those expectations, however, vary according to the child. Realize, though, that those expectations also differ for the individual child depending on content area, concepts studied, and so forth. Remember Betsy from Chapter 1? She studied three different content areas at three different grade levels, each appropriately challenging for her. The fact that a child is gifted in reading does not mean she is also gifted in math. Likewise, a child who is below grade level in math may be at or above grade level in reading. Not only do children differ from each other, but children's abilities and readiness in individual content areas or topics vary as well. Differentiation, founded on appropriately high expectations (and those expectations vary from child to child, from topic to topic), leads to continuous progress.

One expectation that should be held for all classrooms, especially differentiated ones, is critical and creative thinking. Such thinking does not happen in a vacuum. It must be nurtured. Cash (2011) described what a thinking classroom looks like:

- Encourages intellectual independence.
- Recognizes and nurtures brain development.
- Allows and encourages intellectual risk taking.
- Eliminates stereotyping, bias, oppression, and bullying.
- Delays gratification.
- Nurtures social relationships and community.

- Fosters a supportive environment where all learners have choices and a sense of control.
- Builds learners' responsibility for learning.
- Is enjoyable and fun! (p. 94)

His book, *Advancing Differentiation: Thinking and Learning for the 21st Century*, provides strategies and practical ideas on how to develop such a classroom.

Risk taking should be supported in differentiated classrooms. So many children play it safe in the classroom; no one wants to give wrong answers or appear unintelligent. They tend to choose the easier assignments when given choices because success is more likely. But risk taking is necessary (and healthy!) in a classroom where all children are challenged appropriately, when they are learning in their zone of proximal development (Vygotsky, 1978). Too often students mistakenly believe in a fixed mindset regarding their learning and abilities (Dweck, 2007)—they believe they were born with a certain level of intelligence and ability that cannot be further developed, that education is about demonstrating those abilities, and that objective things such as test scores and awards define their success. What they should embrace is the growth mindset (Dweck, 2007), wherein they believe that intelligence and ability are malleable. Through hard work and effort, intelligence and abilities change and grow. Education is a conduit for growth, and success can be determined in many ways—even by learning through failure. Dweck (2007), the cognitive psychologist who coined these terms, remarked: "Success is about being your best self, not about being better than others; failure is an opportunity, not a condemnation; effort is the key to success" (p. 44). A differentiated classroom supports growth mindsets and risk taking; it also emphasizes that failure is indeed an opportunity to learn.

Support Instruction Through Assessment

Assessment plays such an integral role in a differentiated classroom that an entire chapter of this book (Chapter 6) is devoted to it. Assessment must guide instruction. Preassessment prescribes and informs what differentiation takes place, whether that is differentiation of content, process, product, and/or assessment. Formative assessment encourages rethinking the learning and teaching process in order to make adjustments so continuous learning takes place. Summative assessment determines achievement—and, in some cases, even serves as a preassessment for the next unit. Cash (2011) argued that all three must be employed, listing them as one of 10 elements of a differentiated classroom. Please refer to Chapter 6 for more information on assessment.

Support Instruction Through Procedures and Routines

Established procedures and routines minimize the disruption that may result from children learning in multiple ways at the same time. Often, teachers cite classroom management as a major reason why they do not differentiate. Chapter 10 discusses specific strategies and tips that help educators overcome some of these main obstacles facing a differentiated classroom (Beasley, 2009):

- getting started into groups smoothly,
- giving directions for multiple tasks,
- minimizing stray movements,
- starting or stopping in a class or lesson,
- productive use of "ragged time,"
- promoting on-task behavior,
- needing to "finish-up" and "move-on,"
- helping groups work effectively,
- rearranging the furniture smoothly,
- curbing noise,
- keeping track of who is learning what,
- grading daily tasks,
- turning in work, and
- keeping up with on-going papers. (slide 7)

Good intentions and well-developed lesson plans do not necessarily equate with an effectively differentiated classroom where continuous progress for all is the goal. Not only is it important that the teacher design procedures and routines for dealing with issues such as multiple groups and grading, but it is also vital that the students understand and embrace these routines and expectations. Time devoted to this discussion in the beginning is well spent—it saves time and alleviates frustration throughout the year.

Supporting instruction through procedures and routines is one facet of establishing a healthy culture for differentiation. Other important concepts discussed in this chapter include supporting diversity, challenge, high expectations, and risk taking. Not only do these concepts prove essential in themselves to a differentiated learning environment, but they also create a foundation for the final two concepts: supporting a community of learners and supporting excellence in teaching.

Support a Community of Learners

Once students have an insight into their own learning and understand that their classroom is composed of a diverse group of learners, they will welcome differentiated learning experiences. Likewise, once they experience the rush of adrenaline and excitement that comes with successfully tackling a challenge or taking risks in a safe environment, they should embrace differentiation. Procedures become second nature to them as these routines provide a strong foundation for their learning. These concepts help create a positive community of learners where differentiation is the norm.

Cash (2011) delineated five keys to creating a student-centered classroom, the first of which is establishing a community of scholars. His ideas to create such a community included students designing a bill of rights outlining roles and responsibilities. Cash also advocated for students developing conventions that he defined as "agreements, compacts, or standards of practice" such as "all feedback will be constructive to inspire future success" (p. 74). In addition, he believed that an oversight council, a group to deal with transgressions of the bill of rights or list of conventions, should be formed and that the group should practice restorative justice wherein students focus on repairing the harm done by the transgression for the sake of the community. These actions, he argued, would help establish a community of learning in the classroom because all students have a voice and know that their voice will be heard. His other four keys to creating a student-centered classroom should not be ignored; they include building students' empathy and wisdom, developing a supportive classroom environment, developing students' metacognitive skills, and developing persistence, patience, and perseverance.

A sense of community underpins the differentiated learning environment. Students simply don't view themselves as individual learners with needs, interests, and abilities that vary from other classmates. They also see themselves as part of a community that values and supports its members as they work toward the common goal of continuous progress for all. Members have a sense of responsibility for others. They also have respect for them and the learning environment.

Beasley (2009) actually included the concept of community in her definition of differentiated instruction, which shows the integral role it plays: It "is a proactively planned, interdependent system marked by a positive community of learners, focused high-quality curriculum, ongoing assessment, flexible instructional arrangements, [and] respectful tasks" (slide 2).

Support Excellence in Teaching

The bottom line to establishing and supporting an effective, differentiated classroom is the teacher. Period. This was Ginott's (1965/2003) "frightening conclusion"—that the teacher is "the decisive element in the classroom" (p. 15). Educators must expect excellence from themselves and must seek out avenues that lead to excellence.

What does excellence in teaching look like? Gentry, Steenbergen-Hu, and Choi (2011) conducted a study examining characteristics, practices, and qualities of teachers deemed excellent, in part, by high student ratings. Four themes emerged:

- Theme 1. These teachers know and take a personal interest in their students.
- Theme 2. These teachers set high expectations for themselves and their students.
- Theme 3. These teachers make content and learning meaningful and relevant to the future and respect students' choices.
- Theme 4. These teachers have a clear passion for their students, teaching, and for their content. (p. 116)

Effective teachers believe that they make a real difference in the lives of their students, they try multiple approaches rather than giving up on students, and they provide whatever support is necessary for students to meet high expectations (Gentry, 2012). In short, these teachers do whatever it takes for their students to be successful in learning and life. Of course, what works with one student may or may not work with another student, so differentiating is inherent in excellent teaching. However, few teachers enter the field equipped to differentiate.

Educators need a realistic understanding of their ability to differentiate effectively if they are to strive for excellence. One starting point is Heacox's (2009) Teacher Inventory on Differentiation Practices and Strategies (see pp. 13–14 of her book), wherein educators self-assess their usage of various strategies such as preassessment and flexible grouping. Also helpful is her Continuum of Levels of Teacher Development in Differentiation (see pp. 15–18 of her book), which encourages educators to assess evidence of "active, planful differentiation" (p. 15). These tools could and should guide professional growth and development.

When Ohio's Oakwood City School District initiated its longitudinal plan to create and support differentiated schools, the district developed a Differentiation Rubric (Hewitt &Weckstein, 2011), which appears in Figures 9 and 10. As a self-assessment, the rubric encourages the educator to examine both differentiating for interest, readiness, and learning profile as well as differentiating through content, process, or product. Note the thoroughness and high expectations for the distinguished column. This tool, if used objectively and consistently, could transform teaching and learning, as it encourages educators to develop new skills and hone their craft. Of course, the honest self-assessment is the first step. Ideally, the rubric would be utilized during formal and informal observations. The outcomes would then guide professional development. In fact, Oakwood mandates yearly professional development in differentiation. Walking the walk of differentiation and not just talking the talk of it, Oakwood provided differentiated professional development for its educators. Figure 11 is its Differentiation Choice Board, wherein educators customize their learning.

The ultimate goal of professional development is excellence in teaching. When teachers honestly and objectively acknowledge their strengths and weaknesses, especially with regard to differentiation, they are able to develop personal growth plans that include professional development catered to their individual needs.

Concluding Comments

Educators should not be afraid to be the decisive elements in their classrooms, but rather they should be excited about the difference they can make in the lives of their students. They should make children's lives joyous and be instruments of inspiration. This can be accomplished in classrooms that intentionally create and support differentiation.

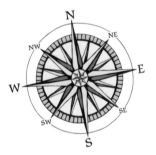

Survival Tips

- Start on day one of the school year. For many children (and their parents), a differentiated learning environment will be a new experience. Communication is key, from using Tomlinson and Imbeau's (2010) opening questions mentioned in the diversity section to sending letters and e-mails to parents.

- After establishing routines and procedures, publish them and practice them! Place charts on the walls that explain procedures or show desk placements for various groupings (more on that in Chapter 10). Practice routines so that the classroom runs smoothly and transitions are almost seamless.

- Set professional goals focusing on differentiation. Do self-assessments using Heacox's (2009) Inventory on Differentiation Practices or Strategies or Hewitt and Weckstein's (2011) Differentiation Rubric (Figures 9 and 10). Try a variation of the Differentiation Choice Board (Figure 11). Ask supervisors or fellow teachers to observe and give input. Differentiation, like any worthwhile endeavor, is not easy—but it is worth it.

Differentiating for…	Domain	Distinguished	Developing	Basic
	Interest	• Assesses students interests (e.g., interest inventory) and uses to inform instruction • Consistently offers students choices for learning • Promotes student interests beyond the classroom • Makes connections between content and student interests • Connects most content to real-world experiences and situations • Consistently plans instruction around student interests • Consistently uses flexible grouping based on student interests	• Has awareness of students' interests • Sometimes offers students choices in learning • Develops student interests in the content area • Sometimes makes connections between content and student interests • Connects some content to real-world experiences and situations • Sometimes plans instruction around student interests • Sometimes used flexible grouping based on student interests	• Lacks awareness of student interests • Offers no choice for learning • Expects students to be interested in content • Makes no connections between content and student interests • Makes no connections between content and real world • Does not plan instruction around student interests • Does not use flexible grouping based on student interests
	Readiness	• Consistently uses pretesting to diagnose student readiness and inform instruction • Consistently modifies curriculum for student readiness • Consistently uses flexible grouping • Uses ongoing assessment data to offer intervention and enrichment/extension as needed	• Sometimes uses pretesting to inform instruction • Sometimes modifies curriculum for student readiness • Sometimes uses flexible grouping • Does some intervention and enrichment/extension	• Expects all students to have prerequisite skills (does not use pretesting to inform instruction) • Teaches to "the middle" (does not modify curriculum for student readiness) • Does not use flexible grouping; groups by "ability" • Fails significant numbers of students
	Strength (Learning Profile)	• Consistently teaches to multiple learning modalities (visual, auditory, tactile) • Consistently integrates students' multiple intelligences into instruction over time (e.g., intrapersonal, interpersonal, logical/ mathematical, verbal/linguistic, visual /spatial, bodily/kinesthetic, musical/rhythmic) • Focuses and builds on student strengths	• Has awareness of student learning modalities • Sometimes considers multiple intelligences when planning instruction • Sometimes builds on student strengths	• Lacks awareness of student learning modalities • Plans instruction without considering students' multiple intelligences • Focuses on student weaknesses

Figure 9. Differentiation rubric: Interest, readiness, and strength. From *Differentiation Is an Expectation: A School Leader's Guide on Building a Culture of Differentiation* (pp. 64–65), by K. K. Hewitt and D. K. Weckstein, 2011, Larchmont, NY: Eye on Education. Copyright 2011 by Eye on Education. Reprinted with permission.

Domain	Distinguished	Developing	Basic
Differentiating through… **Content**	• Adjusts content based on all students' needs to meet standards • Varies teaching and stretches content every year • Provides intervention and enrichment as needed	• Adjusts content based on some students' needs to meet standards • Varies teaching slightly from year to year • Provides some intervention and enrichment	• Does not adjust content based on students' needs • Teaches virtually the same way every year (the content does not change even though the students do) • Does not provide intervention and enrichment
Process	• Consistently uses multiple methods of grouping students • Uses variety of instructional practices (cooperative learning, direct instruction, project-based learning, inquiry, questioning, etc.) • Adjusts rate of instruction and re-teaches as needed • Provides students multiple and varied opportunities to practice skills (e.g., in class and homework)	• Sometimes uses different methods of grouping students • Varies instructional practices at times • Adjusts rate of instruction and re-teaches at times • Provides students some opportunities to practice skills	• Primarily groups students homogeneously by "ability" (uses only one method of grouping students) • Primarily relies on lecture/direct instruction (does not vary instructional practices) • Does not adjust rate of instruction and/or reteach • Provides primarily skill and drill homework for practicing skills
Product	• Consistently uses a combination of formative and summative assessment • Consistently uses a combination of informal and formal assessment • Uses a variety of assessment strategies (pencil/paper tests, performance assessments, etc.) • Bases student evaluation on standards • Consistently provides students multiple opportunities to show what they know and provides students some choices	• Uses more summative than formative assessment • Sometimes uses a combination of informal and formal assessments • Sometimes varies assessment strategies • Bases student evaluation on standards and other criteria (e.g., effort or conduct) • Sometimes provides students multiple opportunities to show what they know • Sometimes allows/provides re-assessments to promote student mastery	• Uses summative assessment exclusively • Uses formal or informal assessments exclusively • Uses one assessment strategy (e.g., pencil/paper tests) • Bases student evaluation largely on criteria other than standards (effort, neatness, conduct, etc.) and does not clearly tie evaluation to standards • Uses primarily one form of assessment (pencil/paper tests) • Tests for concepts and skills one time (does not allow/provide continual assessment)

Figure 10. Differentiation rubric: Content, process, and product. From *Differentiation Is an Expectation: A School Leader's Guide on Building a Culture of Differentiation* (pp. 66–67), by K. K. Hewitt and D. K. Weckstein, 2011, Larchmont, NY: Eye on Education. Copyright 2011 by Eye on Education. Reprinted with permission.

Action Plan (select at least one from each column)			Method of Evaluation (select at least one)
Ongoing PD (be a lifelong learner)	**Collaboration** (work with a specialist)	**Visitation** (get out of your classroom)	**Sharing Out** (learn from each other)
PLC	Reading specialist	Peer Coaching	Create video clip
University course	Intervention specialist	Intraschool observation	Show-and-tell at faculty meeting
Sequence of 4 Pizzas & PD sessions (date/topics will be announced by PDC on September 15)	Media specialist	Interschool observation	Lead a PD day session or participate in a sharing session
	TES (Gifted specialist)	Interdistrict observation	Present at a state, regional, or national conference
Independent or group study or project	Counselor	Co-teaching	Handouts (work samples, assignments, assessments) distributed to colleagues or posted on your website and linked from CIA page
Value Added Learning Network (online course)	Mentor/mentee	Modeling (teach for another teacher)	Write article for Ohio ASCD Journal or another professional journal
Action Research	Grade level team	Webcam/video	Lead pizza & PD session
Independent book study	Department	Teacher walk-throughs	Show-and-tell at grade-level or departmental meeting
Javits Gifted Training	Interschool collaboration (e.g., 6th-grade math with 7th-grade math)	PD Day field visit	Present/publish Action Research findings (on your website with link from CIA page, at a faculty meeting, at a PD day session, etc.)
Online course (e.g., through Ed Impact)	Cross-grade/department collaboration		Curricular Showcase at Board Meeting
Apply for National Board Certification			Share assessment results of differentiated project or assignment with supervisor
Participation in National Board "Take One" Program			Survey students specific to your goal topic and share results with your supervisor
			Create a podcast
OTHER	OTHER	OTHER	OTHER

Figure 11. Differentiation choice board. From *Differentiation Is an Expectation: A School Leader's Guide to Building a Culture of Differentiation* (pp. 68–69), by K. K. Hewitt & D. K. Weckstein, 2011, Larchmont, NY: Eye on Education. Copyright 2011 by Eye on Education. Reprinted with permission.

Survival Toolkit

- Beasley, J. (2009, July). *Establishing classroom routines that support the differentiated classroom.* Presentation at the Association for Supervision and Curriculum Development Conference, Houston, TX. Retrieved from http://ces.shcsc.k12.in.us/Pages/ProfessionalDevelopment/Work%20Stations/1507T_Establishing_Classroom_%28Beasley%29.pdf. This PowerPoint provides a wealth of tips on managing groups and other procedural issues.

- Cash, R. M. (2011). *Advancing differentiation: Thinking and learning for the 21st century.* Minneapolis, MN: Free Spirit. This is a wonderful resource on so many levels, filled with practical strategies and techniques. Most appropriate for this chapter, though, is his approach to growth and fixed mindsets in his chapter on "Problem Finding, Problem Solving, and Decision Making."

- Tomlinson, C. A., & Imbeau, M. (2010). *Leading and managing a differentiated classroom.* Alexandria, VA: Association for Supervision and Curriculum Development. This is a must-have for any educator establishing a differentiated classroom. Note the ingenious strategies for getting to know students' interests, strengths, and readiness levels.

6 Assessment: An Essential Step in Differentiating Effectively

Assessment is today's means of modifying tomorrow's instruction.

—Carol A. Tomlinson

Key Question

- In what ways is assessment the main support system for effective differentiation?

Assessment and differentiation go hand in hand; in fact, they should be intertwined throughout the teaching/learning processes. Information gleaned from assessing students informs instruction, and differentiation targets instruction to individual students, clusters of students, and whole classes. Formative assessment includes preassessment—information gathered prior to beginning the unit. Gathering information via formative assessment ensures that teachers have the means to monitor progress toward standards and/or learner outcomes. Ongoing assessment data provide information teachers can use to match learning experiences to students' levels of readiness, interests, and learning profiles. Without assessment data, teachers do not have the necessary information to provide an appropriate level of challenge for a student or groups of students. Without formative assessment data, teachers plan and implement lessons that often are geared toward the grade-level students in their classes, giving little or no consideration to those students who need extra support to reach the learning goals and to students who already know much of the information or can demonstrate the skills that are central to the unit of study.

Black and Wiliam (1998) defined formative assessment as "all those activities undertaken by teachers, and/or by their students, which provide information to be used as feedback to modify the teaching and learning activities in which they are engaged" (pp. 7–8). Teachers who understand and use various forms of formative assessment can facilitate important achievement gains among their students. Black and Wiliam completed a landmark study of formative assessment that yielded the results later reported by Shepard, Hammerness, Darling-Hammond, and Rust (2005):

> Focused efforts to improve formative assessment provided learning gains greater than one-half standard deviation, which would be equivalent to raising the score of an average student from the 50th percentile to the 85th percentile. In other words, formative assessment, effectively implemented, can do as much or more to improve student achievement than any of the most powerful instructional interventions, intensive reading instruction, one-on-one tutoring, and the like. (pp. 276–277)

Perhaps a way to remember how assessment works in differentiation is to think of it as a theater production. Preassessment sets the stage, as it lets the teacher know where to start. Preassessment is equivalent to the director deciding which actor is best for which part. Other types of formative assessment check for progress of the players (perhaps character development, voice projection, or movement) and find that different characters need feedback specific to their roles. The summative assessment is the actual production, which concludes with the finale.

Assessment in Differentiated Classrooms

Smutny and Von Fremd (2010) detailed key questions with regard to assessment for young students in a differentiated classroom: why, what, who, when, and how? The questions are typical, but the answers direct attention to important aspects of assessment in a differentiated classroom. Assessment must thread its way throughout the instructional process, as assessment informs instruction. This chart in Figure 12 suggests various ways to do this.

Teachers must keep front and center in their planning the fact that accommodating differences is vital and not an "extra" to include if there is time. If

The Learning Journey

Step 1: Know the travelers (children and teachers).

- Are they prepared for the journey? What skills, abilities, and equipment do they have?
- What special problems or challenges do they bring to the journey?
- What differences from cultural background, life experience, and home life influence their ability to embark on this journey (i.e., learn)?
- What do you as teachers bring to this journey (knowledge, skills, experience, interests, resources) and what do you need (what accommodations to your style and preferences, what adjustments due to time constraints and other demands)?

Step 2: Determine the destination (learning goal).

- Where do you want the children to be at the end of this journey (i.e., what do you want the students to understand or to be able to do)?
- What territory (content) will they cover in terms of knowledge gained and skills honed?
- What learning standards and curriculum goals will this journey address?

Step 3: Identify proof or evidence that they have reached the destination (i.e., understand what has been taught).

- What behaviors and comments would show you that the students have reached their destination (achieved their goals)?
- What products, performances, constructions, and experiments would express understanding of the concepts, skills, and information taught?

Step 4: Plan the journey.

- How should the journey begin (what catalysts should be introduced)?
- What teaching strategies should be applied?
- What learning activities should be used?
- What resources should be drawn upon?
- How will the environment be designed and managed?

Step 5: Reassess and adjust according to new needs and changes.

- What are the criteria for knowing that the children have reached the destination (understood the concepts and processes involved)?
- What behaviors and verbal and written responses will reveal that learning has taken place?
- What measures (e.g., observation, questioning, rubrics) will give you the information you need to know if the child is on track or if he or she needs further adjustment?

Figure 12. The learning journey. From *Differentiating for the Young Child: Teaching Strategies Across the Content Areas, PreK–3* (p. 10), by J. F. Smutny and S. E. Von Fremd, 2010, Thousand Oaks, CA: Corwin Press. Copyright 2010 Corwin Press. Reprinted with permission.

schools are all about learning, then teachers must become adept at differentiating instruction. Assessment, both formative and summative, is essential in a differentiated classroom in which instructional strategies are planned to match learner readiness, interests, and learning profiles.

Formative Assessment

"*Formative assessment* is defined as assessment carried out during the instructional process for the purpose of teaching and learning" (Shepard et al., 2005, p. 274). Formative assessment is assessment *for* learning while summative assessment is assessment *of* learning (Stiggins & Chappuis, 2012). The purpose of formative assessment is to support and encourage learning. It includes various preassessments and also other assessments (such as anecdotal records, performances, student conferences, feedback, rubrics, student self-assessments, or work samples) that mark progress toward the learning outcomes. In combination, all types of formative assessments are planned to let teachers better know their students in order to facilitate learning. Data from formative assessments allow teachers to plan and implement differentiated learning experiences that match learners' readiness to learn specific content and skills, learners' interests in general and in specific content and skills, and the learner profiles of students in the class.

Planning Precedes Preassessment

Preassessment is the step that follows planning. Naturally, it is not possible to preassess without planning the learner outcomes. Otherwise, there is no bar against which to measure student performance. Planning always comes first, as it answers the question: What does the teacher want the students to know, understand, and be able to do?

It is critical to remember the three steps for differentiated instruction (see Chapter 1), guided by the following questions (Roberts & Inman, 2009b):

- *Planning Question*: What do I want students to know, understand, and be able to do?
- *Preassessment Question*: Who already knows, understands, and/or can use the content or demonstrate the skills? Who needs additional support in order to know, understand, and/or demonstrate the skills? (Answers to this second question lead to appropriate differentiation.)
- *Differentiation Question:* What can I do for him, her, or them so they can make continuous progress and extend their learning?

"Preassessment makes differentiation strategies defensible" (Roberts & Inman, 2009b, p. 46). Differentiation is a key part of any unit or lesson. However, if teachers can't back up why this child is learning this content in this way, then the differentiation becomes a moot point. Preassessment allows teachers to know why they are differentiating, how to differentiate, and how to meet the needs of all of the students. Preassessment information provides a starting point for each child in her learning in relation to the concept or topic being introduced.

Preassessment or the Assessment of Prior Knowledge, Interests, and Learning Profiles

Students need to understand that preassessment is the teacher's way to take the temperature of the students with regard to a new unit of study—to see what prior knowledge, interests, and experiences they bring to the current unit of study. The results inform teachers about which students need additional support to reach the outcomes, which ones are on target for achieving stated outcomes, and which ones have exceeded the targets and are ready for more complex learning about the concept.

What do teachers gain from preassessment? First, teachers gain valuable information to provide students opportunities to learn what they are ready to learn rather than trying to reach learner outcomes that are beyond their abilities at this time or spinning their wheels on content and skills the students have mastered. Second, they find the misconceptions students have so teachers can correct them and keep students from practicing or reinforcing mistakes.

What do students gain when teachers use preassessment and other types of formative assessment? First, they have optimal opportunities to make continuous progress. Second, they are ready (in both content and skills) to be successful in college and other forms of postsecondary education. Continuous progress prepares them as learners who apply themselves in ways that lead to success and gets them on the path to becoming lifelong learners.

Preassessment to Get to Know Students

The more teachers know about students in their classrooms, the better they can plan to match instruction to children. Gathering information early in the year creates a classroom in which each child feels respected. Of course, learning about children in the classroom continues throughout the school year.

One way to learn about children is through their learning profiles, which should include more than the learning style of students. Tomlinson and Imbeau (2010) described the learning profile as being "shaped by four elements and the interaction among them" (p. 17). The four elements are learning style, intelligence preference, gender, and culture.

- Learning style relates to the students' preferred ways to learn. This element of the learning profile may refer to students selecting kinesthetic, oral, technological, verbal, or written learning experiences. It also refers to students' preferences for working independently or in small groups.
- Intelligence preference refers to the students' desire to use verbal-linguistic, logical-mathematical, kinesthetic, interpersonal, intrapersonal, musical-rhythmic, or spatial intelligence (Gardner, 1983) or to use their analytical, practical, or creative intelligence (Sternberg, 1985).
- Gender and culture combine to create the backlog of experiences that children bring to learning experiences. These experiences differ for all children.

Another influence on learning is mindset (Dweck, 2007). As mentioned in a previous chapter, mindset describes an individual's view of self and talent development. Does he have a fixed mindset, believing that he has talent and just needs to demonstrate it? Or does she view talent as something she has and needs to work to develop? Of course, the second type of mindset, the growth mindset, results in children achieving at higher levels over time. "Without effort, a student's achievement suffers, if not sooner than later. Thus, it is important for students to value and believe in effort as a vehicle for academic success" (Dweck, 2012, p. 11).

Types of formative assessments that are useful with elementary children include surveys to assess interests inside the classroom. Figure 13 is an example of an interest survey.

This interest survey may be the beginning of information gathering to get to know students in the classroom. Later, the teacher can ask other questions that seem important at that time. Getting information in writing allows the teacher to go back and look at it again later on in the school year. Although it seems like this information will be remembered, this is not always the case, so organizing items like this one in folders provides a way to keep track of information.

Information about preferred ways of learning can be obtained in numerous ways. *My Way . . . An Expression Style Inventory* (Kettle et al., 1998) provides one way to learn about student preferences. A page from this inventory is provided in Figure 14. Information from this assessment allows a teacher to learn about how students prefer to learn. (See the complete inventory in the appendix.)

Preassessment to Determine Readiness and Interest in the Concept/Content

Brook Bartrug, an elementary teacher in Hardin County, KY, stated, "A thing to remember with preassessment is that it allows you to see where each

My Favorite Things

1. My complete name is: _____

2. I prefer to be called: _____

3. My birthday is (month, day, and year): _____

4. My favorite:

   a. Color: _____

   b. Foods: _____

   c. Television programs:_____

   d. Places to visit:_____

5. When I have time after school on the weekends, I like to:

   _____

6. I enjoy reading about: _____

7. I have a favorite book or books that I have read more than
   once. What is the title of the book(s)?_____

8. I like to play the following games: _____

9. I have a collection of:_____

FIGURE 13. Interest Inventory.

My Way ...

An Expression Style Inventory
K. E. Kettle, J. S. Renzulli, M. G. Rizza
University of Connecticut

Products provide students and professionals with a way to express what they have learned to an audience. This survey will help determine the kinds of products **YOU** are **interested** in creating.

My Name is: _____

Instructions:

Read each statement and circle the number that shows to what extent **YOU** are **interested** in creating that type of product. (Do not worry if you are unsure of how to make the product.)

		Not At All Interested	Of Little Interest	Moderately Interested	Interested	Very Interested
	Example: writing song lyrics	1	2	3	(4)	5
1.	writing stories	1	2	3	4	5
2.	discussing what I have learned	1	2	3	4	5
3.	painting a picture	1	2	3	4	5
4.	designing a computer software project	1	2	3	4	5
5.	filming & editing a video	1	2	3	4	5
6.	creating a company	1	2	3	4	5
7.	helping in the community	1	2	3	4	5
8.	acting in a play	1	2	3	4	5

Figure 14. Sample from *My Way . . . An Expression Style Inventory.* From "Products of Mind: Exploring Student Preferences for Product Development Using My Way . . . An Expression Style Inventory," by K. E. Kettle, J. S. Renzulli, and M. G. Rizza, 1998, http://www.gifted.uconn.edu/sem/exprstyl.html. Reprinted with permission of Joseph S. Renzulli.

student is so that you can figure out how to get them where they *need to be*" (personal communication, February 15, 2012). This statement provides the rationale in support of preassessment, particularly with regard to content/concept readiness.

Information about students is available from multiple sources and from various types of preassessment, but the key is to gather the information and then to use it to plan learning experiences that allow all children to learn about the same concept or topic but in ways that match their readiness to learn that content, their interests, and their learning profiles.

The clear purpose is to ensure that all children are learning. This type of assessment is important because it monitors progress to make certain that children are neither practicing skills incorrectly nor misunderstanding content. Teachers must focus on learning outcomes, but at the same time they must view student progress toward meeting those learning targets. Just looking forward neglects the need to monitor progress, and solely focusing on the students does not keep a focus on the learning goals. All of the above are important in a classroom characterized by differentiation.

Formative assessment provides information about the level of learning or performance in relation to the standard or target. This assessment allows the teacher to provide feedback for students to improve performance and enhance learning. The quality of the feedback makes a difference in how effective it is for student learning. Just as coaches improve performance of athletes with feedback, so can teachers enhance learning for their students when they provide specific feedback. "Good job" or "well done" does not help students know what to work on in order to perform at a higher level. In addition to giving specific feedback, it is important to provide feedback as soon as possible.

Preassessment results guide teachers in planning instruction at the appropriate level to reach learner outcomes. Leslie Wood, a gifted resource teacher in Butler County, KY, said,

> Preassessment saves time by not going over material with which students are already familiar. That is an enormous waste of time, and preassessment can save us from "stealing" that time away from students who don't need to go over it again and again. (personal communication, March 1, 2012)

Also preassessment prevents giving students learning experiences that are too advanced, providing no anchors for new concepts. Learning must be scaffolded to be appropriate in terms of difficulty and complexity.

In order to be most useful in planning, preassessment information should be gathered early enough to be incorporated in planning differentiated learning experiences.

Pre-assessments should be administered at least one to two weeks before instruction is to begin. They should be individual: the student should complete them in writing (if he or she is old enough), and they should be administered in school. (Rakow, 2012, p. 35)

Preassessments in writing provide documentation of learning progress to share with students and their parents.

It is not enough to plan well, even to plan engaging learning experiences. If the learning experiences do not match students' readiness, interests, and/or learning profiles, they likely will not lead to ongoing learning for all students.

T-W-H Chart: An Example of Preassessment That Yields What Is Known and Shares Students' Interests

One way to gather information is to have students complete the T-W-H Chart (see Figure 15). The T is asking students to tell what they think about the concept or unit to be studied, while the W provides the opportunity for them to say what they want to learn about the concept or topic. The H stands for how the students want to learn the content, giving insights into how they prefer to learn.

The T-W-H Chart opens a window into what the student already knows and wants to know as well as how he suggests learning would be motivating to him. The teacher cannot implement all of the suggestions, but it is a great way to plan to include as many ideas as possible. Including a reluctant learner's suggestion can be a sign of respect that motivates him to engage in learning.

Assessments to Find Out What Students Already Know or Are Able to Do

The goal of preassessing students is to find out what students already know. The T-W-H Chart is one way to do that, but there are other ways as well. When teachers learn what some students, perhaps quite a few students, already know, then they are armed with important information. They can make informed decisions on grouping students in order to allow all of them to make continuous progress.

Punnett square. Four quadrants of a Punnett square (see Figure 16) provide a format for a preassessment on a concept. One quadrant gives the child a place to define the concept, another quadrant lets him give an example of the concept, another is the place to give a nonexample (it is important to know the concept well enough to recognize a nonexample as well as an example), and the fourth allows space for telling anything else he knows about the concept. A

T – W – H CHART

Topic/Unit_____   Name_____

What do you **T**hink about this topic?	What do you **W**ant to learn about this topic?	**H**ow do you want to learn about this topic?

Figure 15. T-W-H chart sample. From *Teacher's Survival Guide: Gifted Education* (p. 91), by J. L. Roberts and J. R. Boggess, 2011, Waco, TX: Prufrock Press. Copyright 2011 by Prufrock Press. Reprinted with permission.

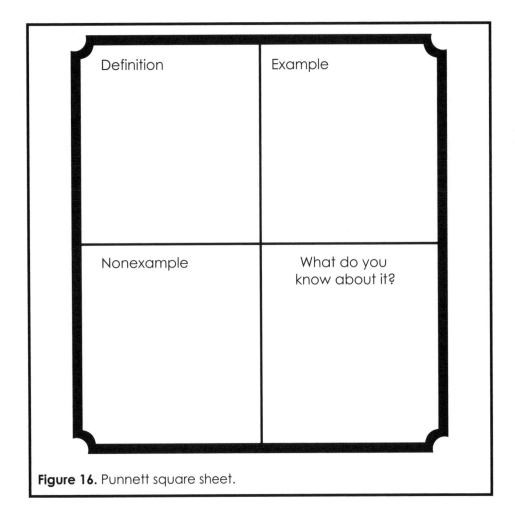

Figure 16. Punnett square sheet.

Punnett square sheet (a template on which the student can write the concept) can be ready to pull out for assessment on any concept.

End-of-unit assessment. There are two ways to use the end-of-the unit test. The first is to use this test at the beginning of the unit. What do students already know before starting the unit? The end-of-the-unit test can also be used as the preassessment for the next study if the content is sequenced.

Of course, these examples are just a sampling of the preassessments available that help determine readiness, prior knowledge, and interest. What they all have in common is that they are written (thus providing concrete evidence for differentiation) and individual (thus informing decisions as to whom needs to be learning what).

Preparing Students for Preassessment

What do students need to know before they complete the preassessments? The first thing to be understood about preassessment is that there are no grades attached, but rather the preassessment provides the opportunity for learners to let the teacher know what they know. They are not supposed to know all of the answers. The purpose of preassessing is to allow students to show what they already know and can do—their prior knowledge and skills. There should be no pressure related to completing preassessments; students should feel comfortable and know that it is routine to complete assessments for each topic or concept to be studied.

Another best practice is to review the content prior to the preassessment if students have studied the topic previously (Roberts & Boggess, 2011, p. 95). Preteaching familiarizes children with the terminology, reviewing concepts they have learned but perhaps have not heard or used recently. Otherwise, some of the students will be placed in a group of learners who need to start at the beginning, yet they will move right along once they make connections between what they are studying and what they already know.

Preassessment as a Time Saver

Many teachers don't really consider preassessment, as they think it would take too much time. Preassessment does save time in the long run. It can save teachers time when they discover that one, a few, most, or all students already have mastered a concept. Teachers save time when they have students engaged in learning. Engaged, motivated children are less likely to have behavioral problems—another time saver for teachers. It certainly can save valuable student time when students are not going over or reviewing what they already know, understand, and can do.

What Does a Teacher Do With Preassessment Results?

After gathering preassessment information, the next step is to analyze it and then use it to plan instruction. Likely, teachers will learn that a few students need support to reach the learner outcomes, others are ready for more challenging learning experiences, and still others are on target for the learner outcomes planned from the standards. Preassessment data help the teacher form instructional groups and determine individual assignments. This information also helps the teacher plan learning experiences that match students' levels of readiness, interests, and learning profiles.

For teachers who give preassessment a try, the results are so revealing that they consider preassessments to be the natural next step after their planning.

Preassessment Guides Goal Setting

An important step to follow preassessment is goal setting. Julie Grim, an elementary English language learner specialist in Bowling Green, KY, described the tie between preassessment and goal setting.

> I know one thing that I always try to do with my learners is goal set after analyzing preassessment. I think it is so important for learners to see where they are and help them make realistic goals about where they need to be and where they should be and where they want to be by the end of a specific time period. It is hard to set goals without knowing where learners are at "that" moment. (personal communication, February 18, 2012)

Goal setting is an essential skill for lifelong learners. Young children can set goals by going over the preassessment results. This information guides the goal-setting process. Self-assessment is important for lifelong learners, and self-reflection can start early in the child's school experience.

Examples of Informal Formative Assessment

Formative assessment continues throughout a unit as teachers use various strategies to ascertain what children are learning. The important point is that teachers are communicating with students to ensure that learning is on track to reach or exceed learner outcomes. There should be no limit on what a child can learn on a specific topic or about a concept.

Stoplight questions. Young children may use cards located at their desks to inform the teacher of what they know and don't know about the concept or topic being studied. Colors of the traffic light are used to answer questions posed to the class. Children holding up red says they have no idea, yellow indicates they think the answer is correct, and green shows confidence they know the answer is correct. This assessment is quick, so it is easily accomplished.

Clickers. A set of clickers for the classroom provides a quick way to ascertain who knows key information needed to proceed with the unit throughout a question-answer sequence. This type of assessment can provide a written record, as well as provide an overview of progress in learning key content.

If you have access to an iPod or iPad cart, eClicker and eClicker Host are excellent apps for pre- and posttests. They allow children to complete written pretests and provide the teacher with instant feedback that is graded and sent neatly to the teacher's inbox.

Snapshot slip/exit slip. Snapshot slips and exit slips provide a spot check on learning. This open-ended "snapshot" provides a glimpse into individual students' understanding of the concept or topic being studied. The snapshot slip is completed during class, while exit slips are an end-of-class assessment. Quick analysis will let the teacher correct misunderstanding and plan next steps for individuals and groups of children.

Self-assessment. Children who learn to think about their own learning are well on their way to becoming lifelong learners. Metacognition should be expected of elementary children, even of young children. Asking children what they learned in the process of completing a project is an important question. Teachers can follow up and ask how the child could have improved what she did and have a better product. Metacognition becomes a habit, and self-assessment is important for students who make continuous progress.

Summative Assessment

At the conclusion of a unit of study or when a project has been completed, assessment is the next step to find out who reached learner outcomes and at what level of attainment. Although formative assessment is assessing *for* learning, summative assessment is assessment *of* learning (Stiggins & Chappuis, 2012). The preposition makes the difference in the meaning of the two types of assessment. Summative assessment is the finale for the unit or project, as it provides the check on what the students have learned during the course of study. This level of assessment may provide important information about the student that will shape further assignments. Teachers may glean information about students' readiness, interests, and learning profile that will add to their knowledge base and help as they guide students in their learning on future learning experiences.

Summative assessments have traditionally been written assessments and are known to students as tests. Certainly written assessments continue to be used in classrooms to determine what children have learned. However, in an elementary classroom, there are other ways to check on what has been learned. Performance measures provide one important way to assess learning. Having children read to the teacher, a volunteer, or a coteacher provides the way for children to demonstrate reading skills. Likewise, children demonstrate skills in speaking, solving math problems, or showing their progress in achieving any number of other skills.

Products provide another means to demonstrate what has been learned in a unit of study. Working on a product is often as motivating for children as it is engaging. Products require hands-on, minds-on work to complete, especially at high levels. Chapter 4 details the use of products in an elementary classroom. Work samples are another way to assess at the end of a unit.

Differentiating Assessments at the Conclusion of a Unit or Project

If groups of learners or single learners have been engaged in different learning experiences, the one-size-fits-all assessment will not be the best way to assess the varied learning experiences. It would be too easy for some and too difficult for others. Right away, teachers may think that everyone will get top grades if assessments differ. If that is a dilemma for teachers, perhaps the question to consider is "What do I want students to get out of this class?" If teachers want students to learn every day and become lifelong learners, then maybe grading is not a problem. In elementary schools, feedback on learning progress is a preferred practice. The Effective Differentiation Model (see Chapter 2) included differentiated assessment for differentiation of content, process, or product.

One way to differentiate the assessment is to offer a product as the summative assessment (see Chapter 4 on products). Products provide ways for a student to demonstrate higher level thinking and creativity with the content as well as with the product itself.

Concluding Comments

Preassessment, one type of formative assessment, sets the stage for differentiating, providing teachers with information to let them know where to start with various students or clusters of students. Formative assessment checks for progress in reaching learning outcomes—which may be different for different students in the class. Summative assessment describes the finale, with this assessment informing teachers of what learning occurred at the end of the study. Each type of assessment is necessary if teachers wish to differentiate learning experiences effectively. Differentiated learning experiences require ongoing assessment.

It is not enough to plan well, even to plan engaging learning experiences. If the learning experiences do not match students' readiness and/or interest and/or learning profile, they likely will not lead to ongoing learning for all students. Assessment informs teachers in making the right match.

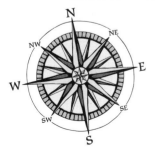

Survival Tips

o Plan and administer three types of preassessments for different units of study. What did you learn about your students' levels of readiness from the information you gathered?

- Use information you gain through preassessment to plan instruction that differentiates learning experiences for students. Remember, everyone continues to study the same concept or topic but at various levels in response to their readiness, interests, and learner profiles.

- Have multiple ways to gather preassessment information and keep the information organized so it can help you match instruction to students. That information is also valuable as you communicate with children and their parents about learning that is ongoing.

- Remember that formative assessment, including preassessment, is not optional if you want all children to make continuous progress.

Survival Toolkit

- Dodge, J. (2009). *25 quick formative assessments for a differentiated classroom: Easy, low-prep assessments that help you pinpoint students' needs and reach all learners*. New York, NY: Scholastic. This is a wonderful, user-friendly resource with ideas that can be immediately implemented.

- Doubet, K. J. (2012, January). Formative assessment jump starts a middle grades differentiation initiative. *Middle School Journal, 43*(5), 32–38. This article provides tips on using formative assessment to guide a school in improving academic success for young people.

7 Common Core State Standards: The Building Blocks of Differentiation

Contributed by Jan Weaver Lanham, Ph.D.

There is no contradiction between effective standards-based instruction and differentiation. Curriculum tells us what to teach: Differentiation tells us how.

—Carol Ann Tomlinson

Key Question

- How and why will teachers need to differentiate with the Common Core State Standards in place?

Standards-based instruction and assessment have become the hallmarks of educational curriculum design as broad-based initiatives established common standards. These standards are intended to be (a) based upon rigorous content with application of high-order thinking skills, (b) consistent and clearly understood, (c) aligned with postsecondary and career expectations, (d) drawn from experts in the field, (e) preparation for success in a global economy, and (f) evidence-based (National Governors Association Center for Best Practices & Council of Chief State School Officers, 2010a, 2010b). As states, districts, and schools work to implement standards-based instruction, fidelity to rigorous content in the context of higher order thinking within a differentiated classroom sets the stage for a classroom with great potential for all students.

Fundamental to the use of the Common Core State Standards (CCSS) is the understanding that these standards establish literacy as multifaceted. Literacy links the skills of listening, speaking, reading, and writing in the context of all content areas; in literary, scientific, and technical fields; and in technology. Within those areas of literacy, the standards identify broad competencies that all students should possess to be college and career ready. It is important that teachers and administrators continue to develop strong knowledge of the standards and learning targets reflected in the Common Core State Standards and that they understand that the term *scaffolding* used repeatedly in the standards means differentiation! The teacher's question then becomes "How will I adjust my instruction, activities, and assessments to assure that my students meet and exceed the standards?"

Start With the Standards

The CCSS are drawn from the set of skills and content knowledge identified to facilitate transition to college and careers. Those standards reflect both broad and narrow expectations that allow and require educators to define specific learning targets and student performance targets. Decisions about grade-level standards and learning targets may occur at the district or state level, driven by state accountability and curriculum mapping. However, the CCSS were developed with broad competencies in mind. The format assures that teachers have increased autonomy in the development of the range of opportunities and experiences they may provide to facilitate standard mastery.

Once learning targets are defined, differentiation is the logical next step to foster learning for all. Differentiation is essential because any classroom of students will naturally include three groups: (a) those students for whom the targets provide the "just right" match between the skills and competencies they possess and the challenge of the task, (b) those students who will require specific supports or scaffolding to reach the target, and (c) those students who have already demonstrated mastery of the basic target and will require adjustment to provide optimum challenge.

Instructional planning begins with selection of appropriate standard(s) to be addressed. Within the context of the standard, the teacher identifies the content through which the standard will be addressed and the student performance and product that equate with mastery of the standard. Once those facets have been identified, the teacher uses student performance data to address three questions:

- Who is ready to address this standard and the identified learning targets?
- Who will need additional support to meet the standard and learning targets?
- Who will need to address this standard with greater depth or complexity?

Once the teacher has a clear picture of the readiness/instructional need within the group, the fun begins!

Standards-Based Instructional Planning

The CCSS are organized under broad umbrella competencies intended to assure student success beyond K–12 education. They were developed in tandem with a set of core competencies that were identified to reflect what a student who is college and career ready should know or be able to do. Those standards and competencies are broad and open-ended enough to allow teachers to use the standards as keys to planning for quality instruction.

A college-career readiness competency such as Anchor ELA Standard for Reading 10—"Read and comprehend complex literary and informational text independently and proficiently"—is certainly a foundational goal for every teacher (National Governors Association Center for Best Practices & Council of Chief State School Officers, 2010a). Tied to that competency is the recurring standard, "Read and comprehend informational texts, including history/social studies, science, and technical texts, proficiently with scaffolding as needed at the high end of the grade level text complexity band" (National Governors Association Center for Best Practices & Council of Chief State School Officers, 2010a). That standard becomes the overarching standard for all reading instruction at every grade level based upon student interaction with text if the intent is for students to interact with that text independently and derive meaning. Therefore, this standard with related learning targets is found at every grade level. See Figure 17 for a breakdown of this standard.

As a teacher addresses this standard, it is imperative to acknowledge and plan for the wide range of reading abilities found in a typical classroom. By beginning with the most "rigorous" basic activities and products possible, the number of students for whom formal differentiation will be needed is reduced and the differentiation strategies incorporated to provide supports can be broadened to reinforce reading and comprehension strategies beneficial for all.

Standards-Based Differentiated Reading/Writing Example

Beginning with two standards—(a) "Read and comprehend literary and informational texts, including history/social studies, science, and technical texts, in the third grade text complexity band proficiently, with scaffolding as needed at the high end of the range" and (b) "Write opinion pieces on topics or texts, supporting a point of view with reasons" (National Governors Association Center for Best Practices & Council of Chief State School Officers, 2010a, Common Core Standards RI3.10 & W3.1)—the teacher plans to use the reading

K–12 Expectation
College/Career Readiness Read and comprehend complex literary and informational text independently and proficiently.
Standard Read and comprehend informational texts, including history/social studies, science, and technical texts, proficiently, with scaffolding as needed at the high end of the grade level text complexity band.

Targets
Knowledge—Identify/
Understand:
• key ideas/details
• craft/structure
• integration of knowledge
  and ideas
	Reasoning—Comprehend:
	• key ideas/details
	• craft/structure
	• integration of knowledge
	  and ideas

Figure 17. Anchor ELA Standard for Reading 10.

selection from the basal series as the anchor literature for the week. Although analysis of the activities shows that multiple standards will be addressed, it is important to begin the planning process with the key standards to be assessed. Through the use of the two identified comprehension learning targets that support ELA Reading Standard RI3.10—(1) "comprehend key ideas and details" and (2) "comprehend the integration of knowledge and ideas"—and the related writing target that supports ELA Writing Standard W3.1—"determine an opinion about the text or topic and reasons that support the opinion"—the teacher builds a set of activities:

- *Day 1*: Introduce story; read independently (some silently with a reading guide and some in guided reading groups); complete story sequencing/cause and effect graphic organizer.
- *Day 2*: Participate in reading stations rotation based on related language arts concepts within the story (figurative language and cause and effect); listening station where students record themselves reading the story and do a fluency self-assessment; vocabulary station; guided reading groups (using basal story or leveled readers).
- *Day 3*: Continue reading station rotation; begin writing activity from the point of view of a story character defending his or her actions (e.g., through journal entries, diary entries, letter to another character); move into guided reading groups (using basal story or leveled readers).
- *Day 4*: Continue reading stations rotation; read nonfiction article about topic related to the story and answer questions. (For example, if the literary reading is a selection from *Because of Winn Dixie* by Kate

DiCamillo, students may be asked to read a nonfiction article about pets or pet care, about the author, about students' experiences moving to a new school, about Florida, and so on).
- *Day 5*: Share and critique character writings; take comprehension test on reading selection.

This sample week reflects a range of activities that are congruent to the identified standards. By using effective questioning in tandem with the student activities, the teacher establishes a set of potentially rigorous activities to address the learning targets and the needs of the majority of students in the classroom. In order to ensure the best match between student needs and delivery, however, the teacher must reflect on student readiness/needs and plan accordingly, as there are students who read and write below level, on level, and above level within the classroom. In order to successfully and efficiently differentiate, clarity about what the student is expected to do to demonstrate mastery is essential.

Based on the standard, the expectation is that students will interact with the grade-level text to derive meaning. However, those students who read below level must have some supports. Reading the story aloud or providing audio texts for read-along with a listening guide can increase access to the text that will serve as an anchor of additional activities through the week. The guided reading instruction for those students would then be differentiated through the use of text at the appropriate instructional level. Additional scaffolding for these students might include provision of instruction of key vocabulary or concepts prior to reading the story to increase access. Additional activities through the week may be scaffolded with Visual Instructional Plans (Jones, 2007), which are illustrated step-by-step instructions that help students navigate independently through multistep directions or processes. Extra support through writing tasks may be provided through differentiated prompts and the use of models, graphic organizers, manipulatives to construct the writing piece, and even a scribe, if needed.

Elementary students who need extra support are the lifeblood of a typical classroom. Teachers tend to intuitively slow down, back up, or reteach when they perceive that a student did not master the standard. Quality differentiation can reduce the need to back up, because the purposeful adjustments made up front keep the student supported while assuring that she is experiencing quality, rigorous standards and activities.

When planning for those students reading above level, the same processes apply, and quality differentiation based on the standards can be designed through some simple adjustments. First of all, a student who is already reading above level will not be served with a standard that focuses on proficiency at the high end of the grade-level text complexity. Teachers must take comfort in the fact that the same standard is in place at *every* grade level, and it is imperative that, for those above grade level, the standard is restated to: "Read and comprehend literary and informational texts, including history/social studies, science, and technical texts, in the appropriately challenging text complexity band proficiently, with scaffolding as needed at the high end of the range."

Adjusting the week for those students who already read above level does not necessarily mean rejecting the basal entirely, especially when there are other classroom activities through the week—discussions, writing tasks, peer review—that require a working knowledge of the literary selection. It does mean that reading selections must be purposeful to assure growth as a reader. The teacher must constantly consider both *what* the students are asked to read and *why* they are reading it. After students have invested time in reading material, the levels at which they will interact with the text will determine whether the reading material and task are appropriate to the standard and whether they reflect growth.

Looking across the week, differentiation for students reading above level might begin with adjusting the literary content of the reading through activities such as reading the entire book rather than just the basal selection, reading a more challenging story on a similar theme, or participating in an author study by reading one of several books by the same author. As the literary selection is changed, the remaining activities through the week are potentially differentiated through that change in content. Each of these options assumes that the teacher has a strong working knowledge of the basal reading selections in order to identify appropriate new reading selections. Good teacher resources included with a basal series often include suggestions regarding "beyond level" activities that can serve as a starting point in the differentiation process.

Differentiation through quality questioning remains a fundamental strategy within instructional planning based upon standards. Reasoning, using inferences, evaluating, synthesizing, and critiquing are fundamental performance expectations throughout the CCSS. Figure 18 provides an overview of a differentiated reading/writing week. The strategies for differentiation developed in the classroom and taught to students should be readily transferrable to other standards and content areas.

Note that rubric-based tasks can be further differentiated through adjustments of the criteria or performance indicators on the rubric itself, including personalized growth indicators that reflect student needs, goals, or interests.

Standards-Based Differentiated Content/Writing

Just as many of the college and career readiness strands and standards for reading are consistent across all grade levels, the writing standards are consistent in kindergarten through 12th grade. The levels of teacher support typically decrease as students' ages and abilities increase, but the high-level expectations

Standard—Reading		Standard—Writing	
Read and comprehend literary and informational texts, including history/social studies, science, and technical texts, in third grade (appropriately challenging) text complexity band proficiently, with scaffolding as needed at the high end of the range.		Write opinion pieces on topics or texts, supporting a point of view with reasons.	
Reasoning Target—Comprehend:		**Reasoning Target**	
• Key ideas/details • Craft/structure • Integration of knowledge and ideas		• Select a topic for an opinion piece • Determine an opinion and reasons that support that opinion	
The student will:	Below Level Differentiation	Beyond Level Differentiation	
a. Complete a book walk using text features to complete prediction graphic b. Read selection independently c. Complete story sequencing/cause and effect graphic organizer	a. Guided/modeled responses b. Read along with audio CD, text reader, read aloud with reading guide c. Modeled responses, sequencing cards, manipulatives to sequence	a. Alternate text—same activity b. Same activity; guiding questions for more complex/lengthy text c. Same activity	
The student will:	Below Level Differentiation	Beyond Level Differentiation	
a. Complete figurative language reading station activity b. Complete cause and effect activity c. Record him- or herself reading selection and do a fluency self-assessment d. Complete vocabulary activity e. Participate in leveled guided reading groups	a. Same reading station activity with VIP b. Same station activity with VIP c. Same station activity with VIP d. Same station activity with VIP e. Same activity with leveled peers	a. Same reading station activity based on differentiated reading selection b. Same activity based on differentiated selection c. Same activity based on differentiated selection d. Same activity based on differentiated selection e. Same activity based on differentiated reading selection	
The student will:	Below Level Differentiation	Beyond Level Differentiation	
a. Continue station rotations b. Write from point of view of character of choice to defend actions c. Participate in leveled guided reading groups	a. Same as second day b. Guided development of graphic organizer prior to writing c. Same activity with leveled peers	a. Same as second day b. Same activity based on differentiated selection c. Same activity based on differentiated selection	
The student will:	Below Level Differentiation	Beyond Level Differentiation	
a. Continue station rotations b. Continue opinion writing c. Read nonfiction article and complete reading guide d. Participate in leveled guided reading groups	a. Same as second day b. Use graphic organizer c. Read aloud, audio CD, or independent d. Same activity with leveled peers	a. Same as second day b. Same activity based on differentiated selection c. Same activity d. Same activity based on differentiated selection	
The student will:	Below Level Differentiation	Beyond Level Differentiation	
a. Share and critique character writing using rubric b. Complete comprehension test on reading selections	a. Same activity b. Test administered with needed accommodations	a. Same activity b. Test based on differentiated selections	

Figure 18. Differentiated reading/writing week.

begin with students' earliest school experiences and continue throughout their schooling. Instructional planning for differentiated content requires decisions regarding both domain-specific (subject/topic) standards and literacy-based standards (listening/speaking/reading/writing). Decisions regarding differentiation within the unit of study must then be based upon knowledge of student readiness or needs within the body of content and within the range of literacy standards addressed.

For example, instructional planning may be based on a social studies standard developed at the state level such as Kentucky's Core Content 4.1 Standard SS-05-1.3.1—"Describe and defend the political principles underlying the U.S. Constitution and Bill of Rights"—and two literacy standards: (a) "Write informative/explanatory texts to examine and convey complex ideas and information clearly and accurately through the effective selection, organization, and analysis of content" (Common Core Anchor ELA Standard for Writing) and (b) "Adapt speech to a variety of contexts and communicative tasks, demonstrating command of formal English when indicated or appropriate" (Common Core Anchor ELA Standard for Speaking and Listening 6). As the teacher begins to plan student products or performances, activities, and the accompanying differentiation, it is imperative that individual student readiness for those activities or tasks is determined through some form of preassessment. Although the U.S. Constitution is not a standard at every grade level, it is addressed annually in all schools in September, making it inappropriate to assume that all intermediate students will know nothing about the topic before it is taught. The teacher must get a picture of student knowledge about the political principles as the basis for the U.S. Constitution and the Bill of Rights. This could be accomplished through questioning with individual student accountability, individual T-W-H charts, a written pretest, or examination of appropriate work samples. The teacher must also use performance data regarding student readiness or mastery of the target speaking, research, and writing skills.

The teacher uses the standards and appropriate learning targets for the grade level to establish basic plans for the instructional week or unit.

- *Day 1*: Read chapter in social studies book; begin small-group activity in which students classify rights, responsibilities, facts, and attributes within the U.S. Constitution and government; begin filling out graphic organizer showing branches of government.
- *Day 2*: Use Constitution booklet to prepare a Venn diagram comparing and contrasting the government under George III and the U.S. Constitution; continue small-group classification activity; begin Boston Plays (Constitutional Rights Foundation, 2010); participate in peer and teacher critique of play performance.
- *Day 3*: Finish Boston Plays; begin letter or speech to citizen of another country describing the roles and responsibilities of the U.S. Constitution

and defending opinions about them (may be early American settler to British family/friend, modern citizen, other).

- *Day 4*: Develop set of questions for Constitution/Bill of Rights *Jeopardy!* game; continue work on speech/letter.
- *Day 5*: Orally share written products for critique; play Constitution/Bill of Rights *Jeopardy!* game in teams.

The week (see Figure 19) represents a set of activities that are both congruent to the identified standards and provide opportunities for all students to explore the concepts of the political principles of the U.S. Constitution and Bill of Rights. Because of the levels of abstraction within the topic and the interpretive nature of the tasks, the basic activities have the potential to provide practice with higher level thinking for all students. However, the activities and products will require differentiation for those students who do not bring the requisite skills or knowledge background to the tasks and for those students who demonstrate advanced knowledge or skill.

When considering the needs of students who do not bring requisite knowledge background to the unit of study, it will be important to differentiate by providing early and frequent access to key vocabulary. Activities with vocabulary and definition card matches or social studies definition games at transition times during the day may be beneficial in reinforcing concepts. Because some of the conceptual vocabulary within the specific unit is abstract, visual/verbal connections should be established and students must be provided opportunity to establish personal connections to the content (i.e., rights and responsibilities they have at home and at school). Students who are not able to read the textbook do need practice with text approach skills, but may need typical reading supports such as audio CDs or text readers. Buddy reading of content texts with guiding questions is another way to increase student accountability to the text when it might be too difficult to read independently. It is important to note, however, that the reading buddy should be a student who is close in ability, as he will have similar instructional needs.

Writing and presentation products may require differentiation in the form of additional concrete supports for organization and generation of product. The use of graphic organizers with feedback prior to writing is essential to supporting students who may lack the skill or confidence to proceed independently. By allowing the students to make major decisions and plan the writing before being faced with the blank page, the teacher makes the actual writing process more accessible. Students with limited presentation skills will require differentiation in the form of personalized cuing, limiting of audience (opportunity to present to a small group instead of the entire class), and personalized presentation rubrics focusing on growth goals.

Differentiation for students who demonstrate strong content knowledge presents opportunity for content adjustment. Although all students must have instruction and practice with strategies to approach a textbook and effectively use text features, students with mastery of the content within the textbook should be given the opportunity to work with more advanced resources, specifically resources that will provide exposure to problems or issues related to the topic. For example, students who demonstrate a fundamental understanding of the U.S. Constitution prior to instruction could be a part of most class activities while working on a comparative study (of the Articles of Confederation, perhaps) or a chronological study of historical changes to the Constitution.

Students who demonstrate advanced writing or presentation skills will benefit from the basic tasks within the unit with small changes to add depth and complexity. For example, the prompt for the speech might be adjusted to ask the student to defend the Constitution to a proponent of a dictatorship or compare the principles in the Constitution to the government of the Roman republic. These tasks would allow the student to use existing knowledge while requiring some additional reading and analysis to make those comparisons. Students with strong presentation skills can be challenged to assume a specific role and support it with gestures, props, costume, visuals, and so on, and the rubric would be adjusted to reflect those expectations.

Standards-Based Differentiated Math/Writing

Just as standards-based instruction in math is a natural fit, differentiation within math instruction is essential. Students come to math with widely varying experiences and understandings, and it is the role of the teacher to identify strengths and needs to design instruction that ensures continuous progress. The standards for mathematical practice form the foundation for all of the math standards, and they establish an expectation of mathematical understanding and application far beyond computation. The CCSS establish a mathematical progression based on full mastery at each level so that new concepts with greater depth and complexity are the focus of each subsequent instructional level. This structure and sequence may pose specific challenges to elementary teachers who do not necessarily know and understand math at the level it will be measured through the standards. Teachers seeking to implement mathematics differentiation may require strategy support; however, implementation of the CCSS in math has exciting potential as teachers experience exploratory changes with their students and gain comfort with those standards for mathematical practice.

When planning for math instruction, it is vital that the teacher look specifically at the standards and identify the learning targets that are a part of those standards. For example, the third-grade math standard—"Explain equivalence

Standard—Social Studies	Standard—Writing
Describe and defend the political principles underlying the U.S. Constitution and Bill of Rights.	Write informative/explanatory texts to examine and convey complex ideas and information clearly and accurately through the effective selection, organization, and analysis of content.
	Standard—Speaking Speak audibly and express thoughts, feelings, and ideas clearly.
Reasoning Target—Comprehend: • Key ideas/details • Integration of knowledge and ideas • Analyze features and impact	**Reasoning Target** • Compose information/explanatory text to supply information about a topic
	Performance Target • Speak to communicate thoughts, ideas, and feelings clearly

The student will:	Below Level Differentiation	Beyond Level Differentiation
a. Read social studies book chapter with reading guide b. Classify rights, responsibilities, features, and attributes c. Begin branches of government graphic organizer	a. Read along with audio CD, text reader, read aloud with reading guide b. Guided/modeled responses; abstract terms may require additional examples or definitions c. Modeled responses, manipulatives to place on organizer	a. Alternate text—same activity b. Student generated rights, responsibilities, features, etc. to classify c. Use existing organizer to develop opinion piece on which branch is most important

The student will:	Below Level Differentiation	Beyond Level Differentiation
a. Create Venn Diagram comparing and contrasting George III monarchy and life under Constitution b. Continue small-group classification activity c. Read and present Boston Plays as simulation of rights represented in Bill of Rights d. Critique presentations using rubric	a. Same activity with terminology starters available b. Guided/modeled responses c. Same activity d. Same activity	a. Same activity b. Same activity with additional attributes requiring more inference c. Write/present original skits to represent each right d. Same activity

The student will:	Below Level Differentiation	Beyond Level Differentiation
a. Finish Boston Plays and critiques b. Write letter or speech explaining/defending political principles of U.S. Constitution and government	a. Same activity b. Guided development of graphic organizer prior to writing	a. Same activity b. Same activity may increase level of difficulty by offering additional comparison to other forms of government

The student will:	Below Level Differentiation	Beyond Level Differentiation
a. Develop *Jeopardy!* questions b. Continue work on letter or speech	a. Same activity b. Use graphic organizer	a. Same activity b. Same activity (may be based on differentiated comparison)

The student will:	Below Level Differentiation	Beyond Level Differentiation
a. Share and critique writing products b. Play Constitution/Bill of Rights *Jeopardy!*	a. Same activity b. Same activity	a. Same activity b. Same activity

Figure 19. Differentiated social studies week.

of fractions in special cases, and compare fractions by reasoning about their size. Compare two fractions with the same numerator or the same denominator by reasoning about their size. Recognize that comparisons are valid only when the two fractions refer to the same whole. Record the results of comparisons with the symbols >, =, or <, and justify the conclusions" (National Governors Association Center for Best Practices, & Council of Chief State School Officers, 2010b, Common Core Math Standard 3. NF. 3.)—represents a dense set of student skills and understandings.

As a teacher prepares to teach this standard, it is vital that planning addresses specific knowledge or reasoning targets that represent the skills and processes that will demonstrate mastery of the standard to be met. The knowledge targets, derived by deconstructing the bullet points representing requisite skills to master Common Core Math Standard 3. NF. 3., include (1) "Explain what the numerator in a fraction represents and where to read it;" (2) "Explain what the denominator in a fraction represents and where to read it;" and (3) "Recognize whether fractions refer to the same whole." The reasoning targets for this standard, Common Core Math Standard 3. NF. 3., include (1) "Compare two fractions with the same numerator by reasoning about their size;" (2) "Compare two fractions with the same denominator by reasoning about their size;" (3) "Record the results of the comparison using the appropriate symbol;" and (4) "Justify conclusions about equivalence of fractions." This standard and set of knowledge targets is only one of several that would be the basis of a unit of instruction on fractions.

As the teacher prepares the unit of instruction on this standard, it will be important for the student to explain, compare, justify, and defend using both speaking and writing skills. Therefore this unit will also include literacy standards that support those skills: (1) "Write informative/explanatory texts to examine and convey complex ideas and information clearly and accurately" (Common Core ELA Writing Anchor Standard 2) and (2) "Present information, findings, and supporting evidence such that listeners can follow the line of reasoning" (Common Core ELA Speaking and Listening Anchor Standard 4).

- *Day 1*: Use fraction circle models to create and record fractions; use graph paper to create fractions as students draw the numbers for the numerator and denominator; use visual models for side-by-side comparison of fractions of the same whole; write a journal entry describing the role of the denominator in the size of a fraction.
- *Day 2*: Use fraction circle models to create and compare given fractions by laying each fraction on top of the other to check size; record the comparison using correct symbol; complete pizza problems with fraction comparison; write a fraction comparison problem for other students to solve.

- *Day 3*: Solve other students' problems, then present and defend the solution orally; play fraction ordering game; given a fraction comparison that has been solved and explained incorrectly, student will write a letter to the student who solved the problem incorrectly, explaining the roles of numerators, denominators, the comparison symbols, and the correct solution.

The week (see Figure 20) reflects multiple opportunities for the students to use hands-on exploration of fractions and comparisons. The need for differentiation through additional support and modeling will be reflected for those students who do not have a solid understanding of fraction vocabulary and relationships. Those students who demonstrate solid understanding of this basic comparison process and fractional relationships will require extension and compacting to assure growth.

The differentiation identified for above-level students in this week would be for students who demonstrate a good understanding of this particular fraction standard, but who need exposure to the related vocabulary and concepts within the unit. If the pretesting indicated that the students have mastered all of the standards within the unit, it would be appropriate to accelerate that student to the fraction standards at the next level or provide meaningful extension activities that allow the students to apply those fraction standards and concepts in genuine activities in math.

Concluding Comments

Although differentiation appears daunting, it is realistic to plan for ongoing instructional adjustment designed to meet the needs of each student. Carefully aligning objectives, activities, and assessments with attention to diagnostic "tweaks" that match the content, the processes to practice the skill or apply the concept, and the performance tasks to the readiness and needs individual students are the practices that make differentiation a reality. Standards-based differentiation is the foundation of purposeful instruction. By selecting standards that reflect high expectations and designing differentiated instruction that ensures mastery of those standards, teachers are able to reach the goal of education—to ensure appropriate challenge and continuous progress for all.

Standard—Math	Standard—Writing
Explain equivalence of fractions in special cases, and compare fractions by reasoning about their size. Compare two fractions with the same numerator or the same denominator by reasoning about their sizes. Recognize that comparisons are valid only when the two fractions refer to the same whole. Record the results of comparisons with the symbols >, =, or <, and justify the conclusions.	Write informative/explanatory texts to examine and convey complex ideas and information clearly and accurately through the effective selection, organization, and analysis of content. **Standard—Speaking** Speak audibly and express thoughts, feelings, and ideas clearly.
Reasoning Target Compare two fractions with the same numerator by reasoning about their size. Compare two fractions with the same denominator by reasoning about their size. Record the results of the comparison using the appropriate symbol. Justify conclusions about equivalence of fractions.	**Reasoning Target** Write informative/explanatory texts to examine and convey complex ideas and information clearly and accurately. **Performance Target** Present information, findings, and supporting evidence such that listeners can follow the line of reasoning.

The student will:	Below Level Differentiation	Beyond Level Differentiation
a. Use fraction circle models to create and record fractions b. Use graph paper to create fractions based on given numbers c. Write a journal entry describing role of denominator in size of fraction	a. Same activity with match me/show me b. Guided/modeled responses; immediate feedback c. Modeled responses, word bank; manipulatives	a. After understanding, begin process of modeling and adding fractions with like denominator b. Journal entry explaining process of adding fractions with like denominator
The student will: a. Use fraction circles to compare; record comparisons using correct symbols b. Complete pizza challenge c. Write fraction comparison problem for other students to solve	**Below Level Differentiation** a. Same activity with match me/show me b. Guided/modeled responses c. Same activity with word bank	**Beyond Level Differentiation** a. Same activity; set challenge to create equivalent fractions b. Same activity c. Write set of real world fraction problems based on comparisons
The student will: a. Solve student written problems b. Present/defend solutions orally c. Play fraction ordering game d. Fraction open response correcting incorrectly solved comparison problem	**Below Level Differentiation** a. Same activity b. Same activity c. Same activity d. Same activity with word bank/models	**Beyond Level Differentiation** a. Same activity with real-world problems b. Same activity c. Same activity d. Same activity with more complex problem
The student will: a. Share and critique writing products b. Play Constitution jeopardy	**Below Level Differentiation** a. Same activity b. Same activity	**Beyond Level Differentiation** a. Same activity b. Same activity

Figure 20. Differentiated math week.

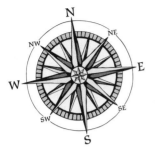

Survival Tips

- Start with the standards. By identifying exactly what you want your students to know and be able to do, you simplify all of the other important decisions you must make in designing instruction.

- Develop a basic plan. By identifying the sequence of activities and student products that will move students toward mastery of the standards, you have developed the platform from which differentiation can be built.

- Consider your three groups. For whom is this sequence and set of activities just right? (You want the majority of the group to be at optimum challenge so you have to differentiate less.) Who will need adjustments or extra supports to master this? (The supports you design and implement will serve more than your target kids and will help you anticipate their questions.) Who can already do this and will need additional challenge? (The challenges you design will also serve more than your target kids, but will help you raise the rigor of all you do.)

- Use questioning. By planning strong basic activities supplemented with rich questioning and writing opportunities, students have the opportunity to work with high-level thinking and processes.

- Have fun! A differentiated classroom is dynamic and student-centered, making it a great place to be for students and adults.

Survival Toolkit

- Heacox, D. (2002). *Differentiating instruction in the regular classroom: How to reach and teach all learners.* Minneapolis, MN: Free Spirit. This is a user-friendly reference for practical application of classroom differentiation strategies.

- Heacox, D. (2009). *Making differentiation a habit: How to assure success in academically diverse classrooms.* Minneapolis, MN: Free Spirit. This is another user-friendly reference by Heacox that allows for practical application of classroom differentiation strategies.

- Jones, F. (2007). *Tools for teaching: Discipline, instruction, motivation.* Santa Cruz, CA: Fredric H. Jones & Associates. This resource offers practical tools for enhancing differentiation in classrooms.

- Tomlinson, C. A. (2000). Reconcilable differences: Standards-based teaching and differentiation. *Educational Leadership*, 50(1), 6–11. This is a great article that may be helpful to other teachers and administrators as you work to build understanding for the need for differentiation in a standards-based instructional program.

- Common Core State Standards Initiative (http://www. corestandards.org): This website is a valuable resource and reference for the standards and supporting documents.

8 A Sampling of Differentiation Strategies

Contributed by Jana Kirchner, Ph.D.

Yes, but . . .
I teach in a four-wall box of drab proportions,
But choose to make it a place that feels like home.
I see too many students to know them as they need to be known,
But refuse to let that render them faceless in my mind.
I am overcome with the transmission of a canon I can scarcely recall myself,
But will not represent learning as a burden to the young.
I suffer from a poverty of time,
And so I will use what I have to best advantage those I teach.
I am an echo of the way school has been since forever,
But will not agree to perpetuate the echo another generation.
I am told I am as good a teacher as the test scores I generate,
But will not allow my students to see themselves as data.
I work in isolation,
And am all the more determined to connect my students to the world.
I am small in the chain of power,
But have the power to change young lives.
There are many reasons to succumb,
And thirty reasons five times a day to succeed.
Most decisions about my job are removed from me,
Except the ones that matter most.

—Carol A. Tomlinson and Marcia Imbeau

Key Question

- Where do teachers start in building up a repertoire of strategies to differentiate instruction?

Too many students. Lack of resources. Not enough time. National and state assessments. Test scores. *Yes*, all of these are very real challenges facing teachers in today's classrooms, *but* . . . teachers can make that powerful decision to create a differentiated classroom where all students have appropriate learning experiences based on their interests, abilities, needs, and learning profiles.

Westphal (2011) described effective differentiation as a teaching lifestyle. She assembled a list of criteria for activities designed for a differentiated classroom. Based on her research and classroom observations, effective differentiation activities possess at least 90% of these traits. Differentiated activities:

- are always based on the content being studied—they serve an academic purpose;
- have a degree of built-in success for all learners;
- meet the needs of diverse ability levels without ceilings;
- are flexible and will grow and change based on students' experiences and abilities;
- encourage intellectual risk taking for students;
- generally have more than one "right" answer;
- provide different ways to obtain and share information;
- ask students to think and stretch;
- accommodate more than one learning style;
- allow for collaboration in pairs, small groups, or large groups;
- allow for a degree of choice;
- accept the students where they are and encourage them to move forward;
- foster responsibility and independence in action and thought;
- allow and expect instructional pronouns to change from "you" (teacher) to "me" (student);
- incorporate real-world applications whenever possible; and
- allow students to move into the highest levels of Bloom's taxonomy and encourage higher level thinking. (Westphal, 2011, p. 5)

This chapter focuses on five strategies that can be used to create this type of differentiated classroom lifestyle that meets the needs of all learners. Each section will begin with an overview of the strategy with examples from different grade levels and subject areas. Survival tips with each strategy will give helpful hints for planning and implementing the strategies, and survival toolkits will provide additional resources for or examples of each strategy. The five strategies are:

- tiered assignments (three-tiered assignments, Bloom Chart, cubes),
- Think-Tac-Toes and choice boards,
- independent study and learning contracts,
- graphic organizers, and
- leveled questions.

Consulting Standards and Preassessing

The first step in planning for a differentiated classroom should always be consulting national and state content standards for the content area and grade level. Heacox (2009) stressed that teachers "cannot even begin to think about differentiation (how we teach, how our students learn) without first considering our standards (*what*) they will learn" (p. 6). The following national standards will be cited in this chapter:

- *Mathematics*: Common Core State Standards for Math (http://www. corestandards.org/Math)
- *English Language Arts*: Common Core State Standards for English Language Arts (http://www.corestandards.org/ELA-Literacy)
- *Science*: Next Generation Science Standards (NGSS) May 2012 draft copy (After revision, the new NGSS standards will be available at http:// www.nextgenscience.org/next-generation-science-standards)
- *Social Studies*: Although national content standards in social studies are in the planning stages at the time of press, each individual content area within social studies has specific content standards for grade levels. These national standards will be referenced for the examples in this chapter:
  - National Center for History in the Schools standards (http://www. nchs.ucla.edu/Standards)
  - Common Core State Standards for Literacy in History/Social Studies (http://www.corestandards.org/assets/CCSSI_ELA%20 Standards.pdf)
  - National Standards for Civics and Government (http://www.civiced. org/index.php?page=k4toc)

After consulting the standards, it is important to preassess students at the beginning of each unit. Preassessments can and should target interests, content readiness, and learning profiles. Chapter 6 discussed a variety of ways to preassess students before implementing any of these differentiation strategies. The key to effective differentiation is to intentionally use preassessment data to match the content, process, or product to students' needs. Chapter 10 explains ways to effectively and efficiently group students when appropriate to aid in managing the differentiated classroom.

Strategy 1: Tiered Assignments

Tiered assignments are an effective strategy to differentiate for readiness level (process; i.e., when some students need more support and practice to master a concept or when some students need more complexity to be challenged). Heacox (2009) defined tiered assignments as "teacher-prescribed learning activities that are specifically designed to respond to differences in readiness, interests, or learning preferences. They are the most prescriptive, learner-responsive, and sophisticated strategy for differentiation" (p. 85).

Adams and Pierce (2011) provided the following directions for making tiered lessons:

1. Identify the grade level and subject for which you wish to write the lesson.

2. Identify the standard (e.g. national, state, and/or local) that you are targeting. A common mistake for those just beginning to tier is to develop three great activities and then try to force them into a tiered lesson. Start with the standard first. If you don't know where you are going, how will you know if you get there?

3. Identify the key concept and essential understanding. The key concept follows from the standard. Ask yourself, "What 'Big Idea' am I targeting?" The essential understanding follows from the concept. Ask yourself, "What do I want the students to know at the end of the lesson, regardless of their placement in tiers?"

4. Develop a powerful lesson that addresses the essential understanding. This will be the base from which you develop your tiers.

5. Identify the background information necessary to complete the lesson, and be sure that students have this information, so that they can be successful in the lesson. What scaffolding is necessary? What must you already have covered, or what must the student already have learned? Are there other skills that must be taught first?

6. Determine which element of the lesson you will tier. You may choose to tier the content (what you want the students to learn), the process (the way students make sense out of the content), or the product (the outcome at the end of a lesson, lesson set, or unit—often a project).

7. Determine the readiness of your students. Readiness is based on the ability levels of students. Preassessment is a good method of determining readiness.

8. Determine how many tiers you will need, using your assessment of the students' readiness to engage in the lesson based on its focus.

9. Determine the appropriate assessment(s) you will use based on your activities. Both formative and summative assessments may be included in the lesson. (pp. 146–147)

Three-Tiered Task

One way of creating tiered assignments is by using a three-tiered task. Heacox (2009) explained that teachers often can meet student needs for a tiered assignment by creating three tiers related to student progress toward the standard: an on-target tier (for most students), an advanced tier (for some), and a modification or adaptation of the on-target tier for students who need more time or scaffolds to move toward mastery. She suggested creating the on-target tier first, then modifying for the other levels based on student assessment data.

Figure 21 shows an example of a three-tiered assignment for a fourth-grade math class. The formative assessment data at the end of Day 1 would be used to determine readiness for tiered tasks on Day 2 of the lesson. Each of the tasks involves creativity and resources students would see as fun (i.e., markers, blocks, construction paper). Students work in small groups to complete their tasks. At the end of class, each group can present its pattern project to the whole class. This tiered activity allows students to learn the same content but in different ways and with different products to demonstrate what they have learned.

Bloom Chart

One way to differentiate learning experiences for students and create tiered assignments is by using the revised Bloom's taxonomy (Anderson & Krathwohl, 2001). Bloom's taxonomy provides a structure for designing assignments at different levels of cognitive complexity, based on students' readiness. All students will learn about the same content but at different levels of thinking and with a choice of different products to display that knowledge.

There are several ways of managing this type of differentiated activity. Of course, preassessing students and organizing work assignments ahead of time are key. One way of dividing tasks is to cut the chart into strips of two (i.e., remember and understand levels), and place those two tasks in a colored folder. Students who need to process the content on those Bloom levels may choose which of the tasks from the folder they would like to do. Another way is to simply cut the Bloom chart into two sections: (a) remember, understand, and apply, and (b) analyze, evaluate, and create. Distribute the two levels to students as needed. Providing rubrics for the tasks will guide students' work and will lead to stronger products. See Chapter 4 for rubric ideas.

Roberts and Boggess (2012) cautioned teachers that one challenge when creating a Bloom Chart is to make sure the learning experiences at the create

Lesson Title: Patterns, Patterns, Patterns

Grade Level: 4

Standard: Generate a number or shape pattern that follows a given rule. Identify apparent features of the pattern that were not explicit in the rule itself.

Steps:
1. Begin by showing photos with examples of patterns: images of sand dunes, pictures of columns on a Greek temple or a local courthouse building, football field, etc. Have students share what they notice about these pictures.
2. Introduce the concept of repeating patterns and model 2–3 examples. Discuss why patterns might be important in understanding mathematics and the world around us.
3. Use a short formative assessment to evaluate student understanding. Based on a quick assessment of their responses, organize small groups for tiered tasks.

Patterns: Task 1: Use the math blocks to create repeating patterns. Have a partner identify and continue the pattern. Trick: Try to design a pattern to stump your partner. (For students who need more practice recognizing and creating repeating patterns in order to master this standard)

Patterns: Task 2: Design a holiday wrapping paper with repeating patterns. Present your paper design to your group and have them identify the patterns. (For students who have mastered the knowledge/understanding level on this standard and are ready to apply that knowledge)

Patterns: Task 3: Design a drawing of the front of a new building that has repeating patterns. (For students who are ready for more complex thinking regarding patterns)

Figure 21. Patterns, Patterns, Patterns lesson.

level really require creative thinking about the content: "Completing a creative product (drawing an illustration or writing a story) does not qualify as a learning experience at the create level, as a creative product can be linked with learning experiences at any level in the taxonomy" (p. 20). Figure 22 shows a second-grade lesson on physical properties of water that includes a Bloom Chart.

Cube

Another way to create tiered assignments is by creating tasks in a cube format. Cubes can be best used to differentiate for ability (process) or learning style (product). Remember that randomly creating six activities or tasks on a

Lesson Title: Water, Water Everywhere!

Grade Level: 2

Standards:
- Obtain and communicate information that water exists in different forms within natural landscapes and determines the variety of life forms that can live there.
- Measure and compare the physical properties of objects.

Steps:
1. Have students complete the appropriate sections of the Bloom Chart, based on their ability and readiness levels.

Bloom Chart: Physical Properties of Water

	Process	Content	Product
Create	Predict	Physical Properties of Water	Story
	Predict what would happen to the environment if one physical property of water did not exist.		
Evaluate	Justify	Physical Properties of Water	Speech
	Justify which physical property of water is the most essential to human and animal life.		
Analyze	Compare/ Contrast	Physical Properties of Water	Venn Diagram
	Compare/contrast the physical properties of water in a Venn diagram.		
Apply	Determine	Physical Properties of Water	Travel Brochure
	Determine where in your city or state that physical properties of water could be found in a travel brochure.		
Understand	Explain	Physical Properties of Water	PowerPoint Presentation
	Explain physical properties of water in a PowerPoint presentation.		
Remember	Identify	Physical Properties of Water	Chart or Pictures
	Identify physical properties of water in a chart or with pictures.		

Figure 22. Water, Water Everywhere! lesson.

cube and having students roll the cube, then requiring them to complete that task is *not* differentiation. Differentiation involves intentionally varying the content, process, or product to meet students' needs. If there is not an intentional match between the task and the student, then, although rolling the cube may be engaging to students as an activity, it is not differentiating. For example, a cube commonly seen in classrooms has six components that can be used with a concept: apply it, analyze it, describe it, argue for or against it, associate it, and compare it. Although these do represent several Bloom's levels, if the roll of the cube is random, there is no intentional match between the student and the cognitive level of the task. This cube activity would be better used as a fun discussion starter than as a differentiated lesson.

The examples of cubes in Figure 23 are for a unit on E. B. White's *Charlotte's Web* in a third-grade class. After reading the novel, these cubes could be used as a learning activity that allows students to process events from the novel to aid in their reading comprehension or as a formative assessment.

Based on knowledge of students' learning styles, the teacher would group the students and give each group one of the three cubes (copied on different color paper). Each of the cubes allows students to demonstrate their content knowledge in their learning style preference. Cube 1 is an example of a cube that could be used to differentiate for kinesthestic learners. Cube 2 is the same content, but all of the products on this cube are visual products. Cube 3 has choices that are all linguistic in nature. The content is the same (examining a scene), but there are six different products per learning style or per cube. Having students roll their assigned cube and complete the task from their roll is an intentional match of student and learning style preference.

Another approach to differentiating with cubes is to level the tasks on the cube by student readiness or ability (differentiating by process). Using the same *Charlotte's Web* unit, the teacher would assess students on their understanding of the book first in order to organize the groups. Figure 24 shows a cube with lower level tasks, and Figure 25 shows a cube with more challenging tasks. Once again, the content is the same (e.g., plot, writing techniques, conflict, theme). Students could roll the cube and work on the task with a partner. Each small group could share its work and report its findings to the whole class.

Lesson Title: Exploring *Charlotte's Web*

Grade Level: 3

Standards:
- Ask and answer questions to demonstrate understanding of a text, referring explicitly to the text as the basis for the answers.
- Describe characters in a story (e.g., their traits, motivations, or feelings) and explain how their actions contribute to the sequence of events.
- Refer to parts of stories, dramas, and poems when writing or speaking about a text, using terms such as chapter, scene, and stanza; describe how each successive part builds on earlier sections.
- Distinguish their own point of view from that of the narrator or those of the characters.

Steps:
1. Use these cubes after students have finished reading the novel. Based on knowledge of students' learning styles, the teacher will group the students.
2. Give each group one of the three cubes (copied on different color paper).
3. Have the students complete the tasks on the cube.

Figure 23. *Charlotte's Web* lesson.

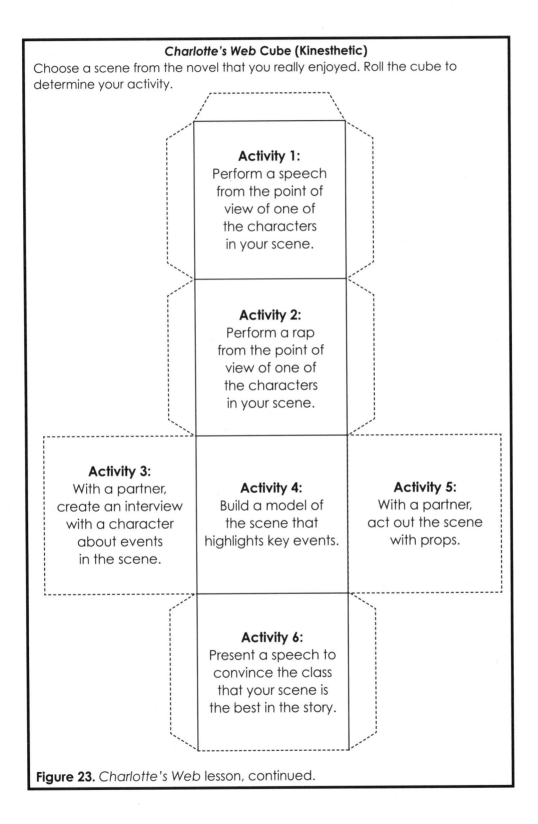

Figure 23. *Charlotte's Web* lesson, continued.

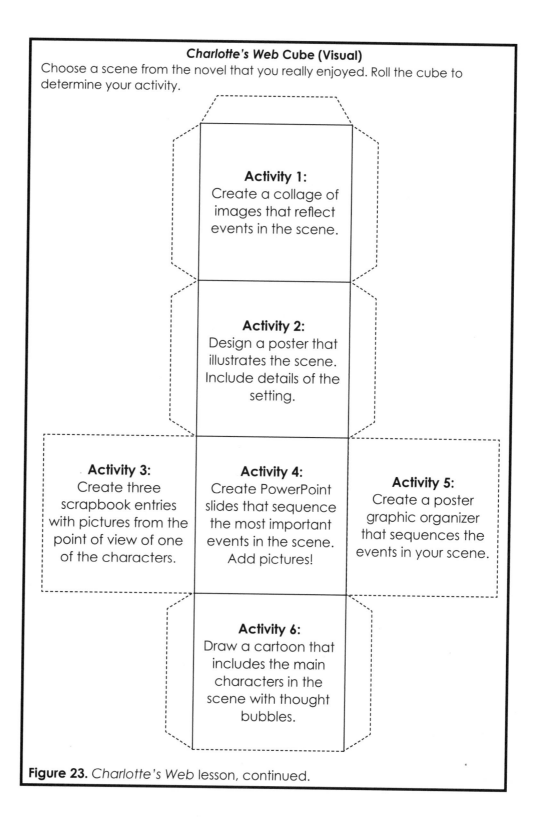

Figure 23. *Charlotte's Web* lesson, continued.

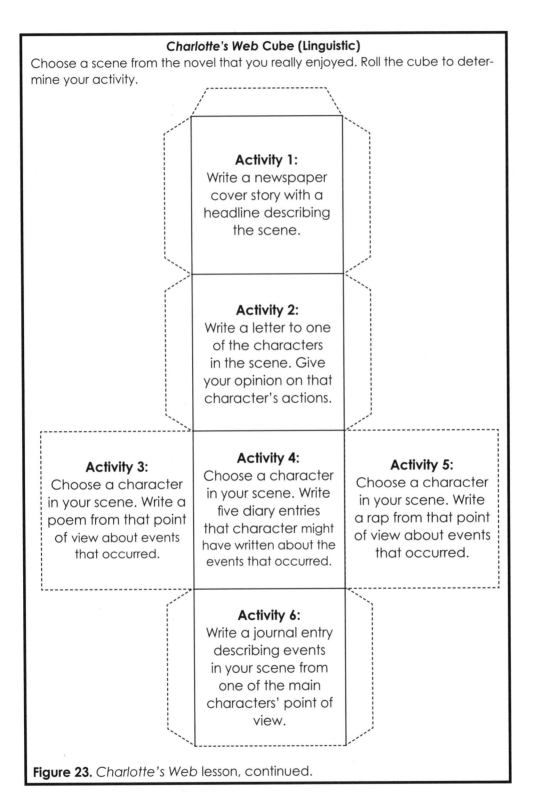

***Charlotte's Web* Cube (Linguistic)**

Choose a scene from the novel that you really enjoyed. Roll the cube to determine your activity.

Activity 1:
Write a newspaper cover story with a headline describing the scene.

Activity 2:
Write a letter to one of the characters in the scene. Give your opinion on that character's actions.

Activity 3:
Choose a character in your scene. Write a poem from that point of view about events that occurred.

Activity 4:
Choose a character in your scene. Write five diary entries that character might have written about the events that occurred.

Activity 5:
Choose a character in your scene. Write a rap from that point of view about events that occurred.

Activity 6:
Write a journal entry describing events in your scene from one of the main characters' point of view.

Figure 23. *Charlotte's Web* lesson, continued.

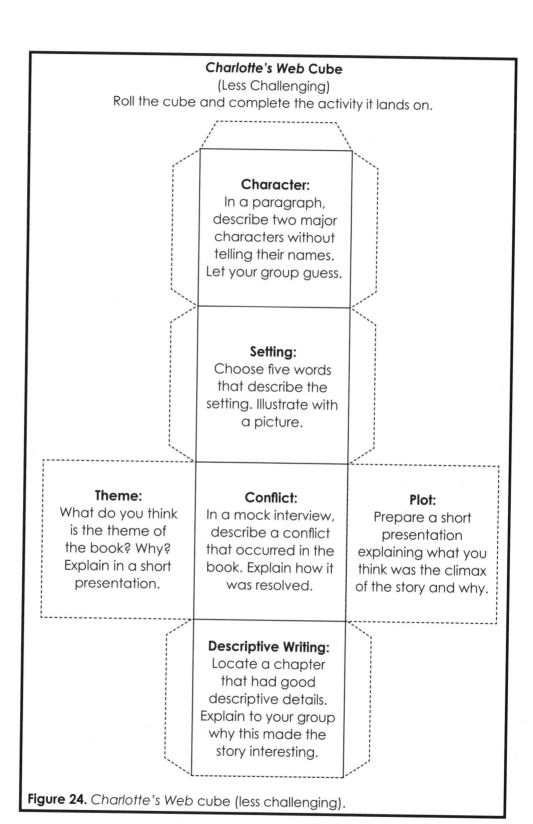

Charlotte's Web Cube
(Less Challenging)
Roll the cube and complete the activity it lands on.

Character:
In a paragraph, describe two major characters without telling their names. Let your group guess.

Setting:
Choose five words that describe the setting. Illustrate with a picture.

Theme:
What do you think is the theme of the book? Why? Explain in a short presentation.

Conflict:
In a mock interview, describe a conflict that occurred in the book. Explain how it was resolved.

Plot:
Prepare a short presentation explaining what you think was the climax of the story and why.

Descriptive Writing:
Locate a chapter that had good descriptive details. Explain to your group why this made the story interesting.

Figure 24. *Charlotte's Web* cube (less challenging).

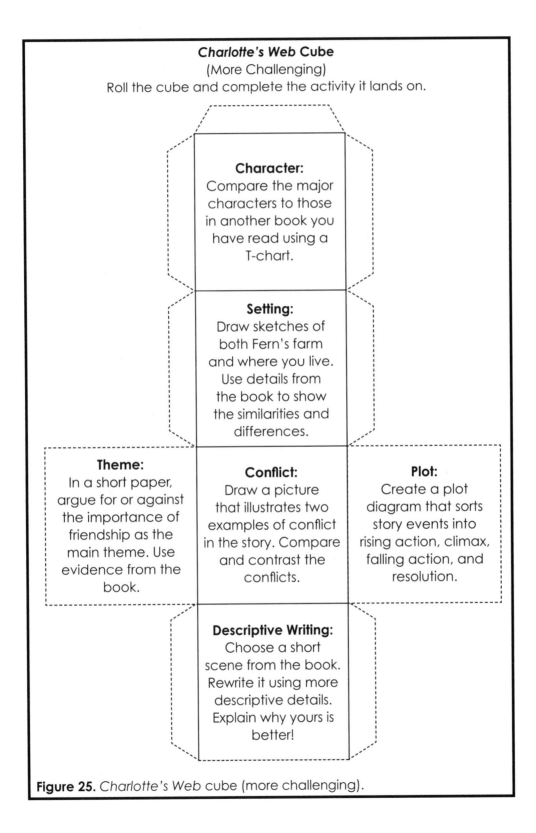

Figure 25. *Charlotte's Web* cube (more challenging).

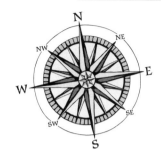

Survival Tips

Criteria for Well-Designed Tiered Assignments

- Are used as necessary and appropriate to address the learning differences in the classroom.

- Are clearly focused on learning goals.

- Reflect work on critical content, processes, or skills.

- Are designed to respond to the immediate and specific learning needs of different groups of students (i.e., tiered by readiness, challenge and complexity, degree of structure, level of abstraction, learning preference, or need for support).

- Are equally active, engaging, and interesting.

- Reflect differences in purpose and are not simply more or less redundant work.

- Require similar time commitments.

- Either all can be completed during the class period or all require homework.

- May be assigned to be completed individually, with a partner with like needs, or collaboratively in a small group of like learners.

- Offer an opportunity for students to learn from each other. Tiers should offer different but related experiences. Students should share their work.

- Are used as practice or daily work, not as an assessment to be graded. (Heacox, 2009, p. 87)

Survival Toolkit

- Adams, C.M., & Pierce, R.L. (2011). *Differentiation that really works: Strategies from real teachers for real classrooms (grades K–2).* Waco, TX: Prufrock Press. This book provides examples of several differentiation strategies and examples for grades K–2.

- Conklin, W. (2010). *Differentiation strategies for social studies.* Huntington Beach, CA: Shell Education. This resource has examples of tiered assignments for all grade levels in social studies.

- Heacox, D. (2009). *Making differentiation a habit*. Minneapolis, MN: Free Spirit. This resource provides an overview of several different strategies for differentiating instruction.

- Parker, C. (2007). *Applying differentiation strategies*. Huntington Beach, CA: Shell Education. This is another great resource that includes a variety of differentiation strategies with specific content examples.

- Sower, J., & Warner, L. (2011). *Differentiating instruction with centers in the inclusive classroom*. Waco, TX: Prufrock Press. This resource describes centers that are used to differentiate in primary classrooms.

- Cube Creator (http://www.readwritethink.org/files/resources/interactives/cube_creator): This page provides an interactive cube creator for a story, mystery, biography, or other topic.

- Dice Maker (http://www.toolsforeducators.com/dice): This site allows you to create dice to use in the cubing strategy.

- Tools for Differentiation (http://toolsfordifferentiation.pbworks.com/w/page/22360094/FrontPage): This wiki contains information and examples of differentiated strategies created by teachers.

Strategy 2: Think-Tac-Toe and Choice Boards

Think-Tac-Toes, or choice boards, are another way of creating effective differentiated learning experiences for students. Usually organized in a 3 x 3 or 4 x 4 grid, Think-Tac-Toes often have a label column on the left side. After a unit on ancient Egypt, for example, teachers could create a Think-Tac-Toe with these headings on the first column: culture, religion, achievements, and important leaders. Students could pick one task from each of the rows to show their content knowledge on each of these subtopics in the unit. Students do not have to complete a row (as in a traditional tic-tac-toe game) but rather should be allowed to choose their products under each topic. It is also important to offer choices of products within the squares that differentiate for different learning styles (i.e., visual, kinesthetic, linguistic, etc.).

Figure 26 shows a geometry Think-Tac-Toe that is appropriate for a kindergarten class and differentiates for learning styles based on Gardner's (1983) multiple intelligences. Students choose one product from each row:

- Two-dimensional shapes
- Three-dimensional shapes
- Name that shape!

Think-Tac-Toes or choice boards can also be used to differentiate for students' ability levels; in fact, this is the best approach to ensure appropriate challenge for students. Conklin (2010) used shapes placed in the individual squares of the choice board to differentiate for students' ability. For instance, students who are on grade level choose any tasks with a square in the corner of the box, above-grade-level students choose from boxes with triangles, below-grade-level students choose from boxes with circles, and English language learners choose from boxes with stars.

Teachers can also provide two separate Think-Tac-Toe charts based on students' ability levels. The fifth-grade example in Figure 27 shows how to level the Think-Tac-Toes for students. Results of formative assessments mid-unit would allow the teacher to sort students and provide the appropriate Think-Tac-Toe to each group or individual. Students would still be allowed choice within their respective charts.

Keep in mind the following background information for the lesson in Figure 27: In a fifth-grade unit on Westward Expansion in the United States, students have examined the events during this era from the perspective of three different groups: Native Americans, pioneers, or railroad investors. Throughout the unit, both whole-group instruction and individual learning centers with maps, primary sources, secondary sources, and artwork were provided for students to

Lesson Title: Exploring Shapes

Grade Level: Kindergarten

Standards:
- Analyze and compare two- and three-dimensional shapes, in different sizes and orientations, using informal language to describe their similarities, differences, parts (e.g., number of sides and vertices/"corners") and other attributes (e.g., having sides of equal length).
- Model shapes in the world by building shapes from components (e.g., sticks and clay balls) and drawing shapes.
- Compose simple shapes to form larger shapes.

Steps:
1. Students choose one product from each row to complete after finishing their study of geometry.

Two-Dimensional Shapes	Write or record (using an iPad) a journal entry from a day in the life of a 2D shape. Make sure to include its characteristics. (Verbal)	Create a new large shape made up of smaller 2D shapes. (Visual)	Draw a poster that includes five examples of 2D shapes. (Visual)
Three-Dimensional Shapes	Write and perform a rap that explains the characteristics of 3D shapes. (Musical)	Build a 3D shape out of arts and crafts materials located in the room. Be ready to prove your creation is three-dimensional. (Visual, Kinesthetic)	Create a presentation showing and naming as many 3D shapes as possible (options: PowerPoint, Prezi, etc.). (Visual)
Name That Shape!	Locate as many shapes as possible throughout the school building. Design a map that pinpoints the location and name of these shapes. (Kinesthetic/Visual)	Design a building plan for a new playground. Include as many shapes as possible! Make sure to label them. (Visual)	Choose two shapes we have studied. Write or record a short story from one shape to another explaining why one shape is so popular! (Verbal)

Figure 26. Exploring Shapes Think-Tac-Toe and lesson.

research and to answer this essential question from their group's point of view: Was Westward Expansion good for the United States?

The Think-Tac-Toes for Figure 27 would be used as a formative assessment as the unit progresses. Students will choose two of the three possible choices of products (differentiation by product) to display their knowledge of events from their point of view. The content is the same, as they all have studied maps, images, paintings, and other primary sources. These Think-Tac-Toes are also differentiated by ability level or process. The Think-Tac-Toe with the train graphic has less challenging tasks than those in the Think-Tac-Toe with the mountains graphic. In a quick, easy way, the teacher can present the Think-Tac-Toe assignments to individual students based on their readiness for the task complexity.

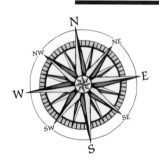

Survival Tips

- Developing rubrics for student products is critical to encourage quality products. Roberts and Inman (2009a) created the Developing and Assessing Products (DAP) Tool as a way to assess student products in a consistent way based on four categories: content, presentation, creativity, and reflection. Check out their book, *Assessing Differentiated Student Products*, for examples of tiered DAP Tools for posters, PowerPoints, collages, presentations, masks, interviews, movies, and much more.

Survival Toolkit

- Karnes, F. A., & Stephens, K. R. (2009). *The ultimate guide for student product development and evaluation* (2nd ed.). Waco, TX: Prufrock Press. This resource provides a thorough list of student products with scoring criteria and resources needed for each product.

- Roberts, J. L., & Inman, T. F. (2009). *Assessing differentiated student products: A protocol for development and evaluation.* Waco, TX: Prufrock Press. This book is an excellent resource for tiered or differentiated scoring guides for a variety of student products.

- Kathy Schrock's Guide to Everything: Assessment and Rubrics (http://www.schrockguide.net/assessment-and-rubrics.html): This page houses Kathy Schrock's collection of rubrics.

- Rubistar (http://rubistar.4teachers.org): This is a rubric development site.

Lesson Title: America Travels West

Grade Level: 5

Standards:

- *National History Standard:* Understand the settlement of the West
- *Common Core Reading/Writing History Standard:* Analyze multiple accounts of the same event or topic, noting important similarities and differences in the point of view they represent

Steps:

1. After studying Westward Expansion, students will aim to answer the question, "Was Westward Expansion good for the United States?" by completing tasks found in the Think-Tac-Toes below.
2. From the Think-Tac-Toes, students will choose two of the three possible choices of products (differentiation by product) to display their knowledge of events from their point of view.

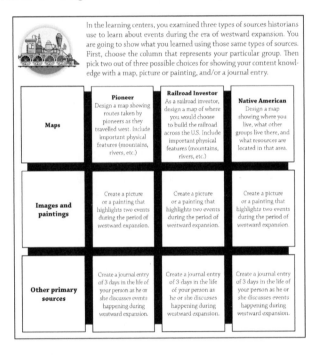

Figure 27. Westward Expansion lesson. From *Differentiating Instruction With Centers in the Gifted Classroom* (pp. 69–70), by J. L. Roberts and J. R. Boggess, 2012, Waco, TX: Prufrock Press. Copyright 2012 by Prufrock Press. Reprinted with permission.

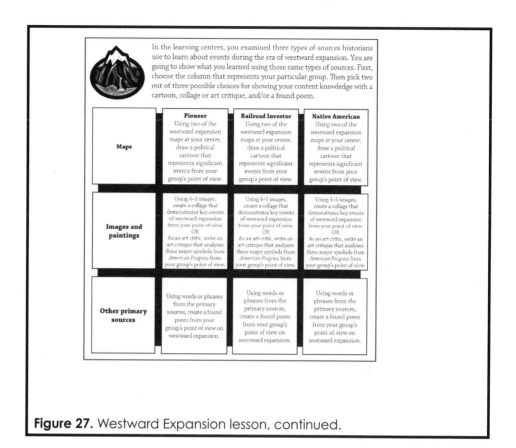

In the learning centers, you examined three types of sources historians use to learn about events during the era of westward expansion. You are going to show what you learned using those same types of sources. First, choose the column that represents your particular group. Then pick two out of three possible choices for showing your content knowledge with a cartoon, collage or art critique, and/or a found poem.

	Pioneer	Railroad Investor	Native American
Maps	Using two of the westward expansion maps at your center, draw a political cartoon that represents significant events from your group's point of view.	Using two of the westward expansion maps at your center, draw a political cartoon that represents significant events from your group's point of view.	Using two of the westward expansion maps at your center, draw a political cartoon that represents significant events from your group's point of view.
Images and paintings	Using 4–5 images, create a collage that demonstrates key events of westward expansion from your point of view. OR As an art critic, write an art critique that analyzes three major symbols from *American Progress* from your group's point of view.	Using 4–5 images, create a collage that demonstrates key events of westward expansion from your point of view. OR As an art critic, write an art critique that analyzes three major symbols from *American Progress* from your group's point of view.	Using 4–5 images, create a collage that demonstrates key events of westward expansion from your point of view. OR As an art critic, write an art critique that analyzes three major symbols from *American Progress* from your group's point of view.
Other primary sources	Using words or phrases from the primary sources, create a found poem from your group's point of view on westward expansion.	Using words or phrases from the primary sources, create a found poem from your group's point of view on westward expansion.	Using words or phrases from the primary sources, create a found poem from your group's point of view on westward expansion.

Figure 27. Westward Expansion lesson, continued.

Strategy 3: Independent Study and Learning Contracts

Independent projects are an excellent way to differentiate for content, process, and product. Within the context of the standard, students can be allowed to choose an aspect of the content topic and develop their own project and plan. For instance, in an elementary class studying the effects of the Civil War, students could choose an aspect of the war they find most interesting such as the life of a soldier, nurses and medicine, battles, military tactics, military leaders, or life in a prison camp. By allowing students a choice in not only developing their research and work plan, but also in choosing the product to display their knowledge, they develop an ownership and increased motivation to do the work.

Cash (2011) referred to student-chosen topics as "passion projects" (p. 54), which emphasizes the intensity of interest possible. Stanley (2012) described the critical element of student project-based learning (PBL) as follows:

Although there are many variables that can be changed within PBL—from the amount of time students have, to the resources they are given, to the product and so on—what always remains the same is that students are given the majority of the responsibility for their own learning. (p. 2)

With independent study, students are given the responsibility to choose a topic, prioritize the tasks, manage their time, and choose their products, all 21st-century skills.

The key to managing the classroom with a variety of independent projects occurring at the same time is to include personal agenda planners, goal-setting, learning contracts, and/or progress reports. Cash (2011) suggested having students set specific, measurable, attainable, relevant, and time-bound (SMART) goals and keep reflection logs of their progress. Stanley (2012) and Winebrenner (2001) suggested independent study project contracts that include a student's project topic, goals, skills learned, work plan, resources needed and/or used, and student, teacher, and parent signatures.

As with any product created by students, it is important to have rubrics to guide the product development. Roberts and Inman (2009a) shared a variety of DAP Tools tiered into levels based on the student's experience with the product. These DAP Tools also include a student self-reflection piece that is often missing in rubrics. Rubrics should be shared with students as they work on the project and product. The teacher's role becomes that of a facilitator by providing assistance, resources, and support as needed.

Figure 28 is a third-grade unit called Myths From Around the World. The standards require students to tell the stories, determine the moral or lesson taught, and compare and contrast themes and events. By adding the research standard in the independent project, students will be able to practice research skills. Teachers would definitely want to model the task with one culture and myth before they began their independent work. It would also be useful to brainstorm a list of all of the possible products available to demonstrate their learning. Having students label a world map and create a timeline would help them develop background knowledge about the "when and where" of different cultures around the world.

Students could also be allowed to work with a partner to develop goals and a plan for the research and project design. Winebrenner (2001) encouraged a Resident Expert Planner model that has students develop questions for their topic, begin taking notes, track their resources, identify supplies needed, log their work, and troubleshoot problems. Figure 28 shows the lesson and the sample task sheet or agenda that could be given to students.

The next example, Figure 29, shows a way to integrate the study of animals and habitats with research skills and literacy strategies for reading informational

Lesson Title: Myths From Around the World

Grade Levels: 3–4

Standards:

- (Grade 3) Recount stories, including fables, folktales, and myths from diverse cultures; determine the central message, lesson, or moral and explain how it is conveyed through key details in the text.
- (Grade 4) Compare and contrast the treatment of similar themes and topics (e.g., opposition of good and evil) and patterns of events (e.g., the quest) in stories, myths, and traditional literature from different cultures.
- Conduct short research projects that build knowledge through investigation of different aspects of a topic.

Steps:

1. Give students the task sheet on the following page as they begin their independent study of myths and stories from other cultures.
2. Students should make sure they cover the Important Tasks section of the sheet after choosing a culture to study.
3. Meet periodically with the students to check in on their progress.

Research Project and Presentation: Myths From Around the World

All cultures and people around the world have stories to explain the things that are important to them. They may be called myths, fables, legends, or folktales, but they all explain something about what the people or that culture valued.

Your task is to choose a culture, research a myth from that culture, and present your findings in a product of your choice.

Important Tasks:

- Retell the major events in the story.
- Answer the question of "Who are the major characters?"
- Answer the question of "What is the moral or lesson?"
- Provide background on the culture you've chosen (such as time period, location, and interesting facts about the culture that tie into the myth).
- Explain how this myth reflects the culture. For example, what elements in the myth make it Egyptian or Norse?
- Create your own product to show the class what you have learned.

You will have meetings with the teacher during your research time to check your progress on your goals and work plan.

Figure 28. Myths From Around the World lesson.

Possible Places:
- India
- China
- Japan
- Greece
- Rome
- Vikings (Norse)
- Africa (may choose one particular country)
- Egypt
- Native Americans (may choose one group; e.g., Cherokee)
- Australia
- Central or South America

Possible Sources:
- http://teacher.scholastic.com/writewit/mff/myths.htm
- http://www.unc.edu/~rwilkers/title.htm

Figure 28. Myths From Around the World lesson, continued.

texts in a third-grade classroom. As with the previous example, it is important for the teacher to help generate ideas, model the process of collecting information, conduct whole-group mini-lessons as needed, help brainstorm product choices, and provide rubrics for student work. This assignment differentiates for student interests and products, as students get to choose their animal example.

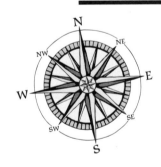

Survival Tips

- In *Differentiation Made Simple: Timesaving Tools for Teachers,* Carr (2009) provided the following steps as a guide to help students get started on a research project:

  O Choose a topic to research.

  O Write down everything you already know about this topic on index cards or a sheet of notebook paper. Then, write down all of the things you think you know about this topic, but are not certain are correct.

  O Make a list of questions you have about your research topic. Try to think of questions that are *open-ended,* questions that cannot be answered with just one or two words.

  O Choose three good open-ended questions and write them on note cards. Clip the cards to the envelopes

Lesson Title: Animal Habitats at the Zoo

Grade Level: 3

Standards:

- *Science Standards: Category: Environmental Impact on Organisms:*
  - o Obtain, evaluate, and communicate information about the types of habitats in which organisms live, and ask questions based on that information.
  - o Use data about the characteristics of organisms and habitats to design an artificial habitat in which the organisms can survive.

- *Reading Standards—Informational Text:*
  - o Ask and answer questions to demonstrate understanding of a text, referring explicitly to the text as the basis for the answers.

Steps:

1. Read the prompt below to students, then give them the agenda sheet to complete their independent study.
2. Meet with students periodically to check their progress.

Animal Habitats at the Zoo

Congratulations! You have been chosen as an animal expert and given the task of creating a home for your animal at the local zoo. This job is very important because the animal's life depends on your good choices about what it needs to survive. You must design a habitat for your animal and present that habitat to the Zoo Board (our class) with an explanation of why it will work for your animal.

Steps:

1. Brainstorm a list of your favorite animals. Rank the animals 1–5 (1 being your favorite), and the teacher will help you select an animal that will be the focus of your research.
2. Your first task is to research important details about that animal to be able to design its habitat. Start with making a list of all of the questions you might need to know about your animal. Resources in the classroom, library, and computer lab will be available to you.
3. Your final task will be to create a habitat for your animal and present it to the class. You may choose how you would like to present your project (a PowerPoint, model, poster drawings, etc.).
4. You will design a work plan to make sure you are ready by presentation day.
5. Rubrics will be provided so you can make sure to check yourself and do your best work.

Figure 29. Animal Habitats at the Zoo lesson.

in the folder—one question per card and one card per envelope.

○ Research the questions. Use a variety of resources to help you find the answers to the questions. As you read, jot down facts on index cards—one fact per card—that give details regarding the questions. . . . Put all of these cards inside the envelope for this question. Then, turn your attention to the question on the next envelope and repeat the directions. . . (p. 113)

⦿ Remember to allow student choice in topic and product whenever possible.

Survival Toolkit

⦿ Carr, M. A. (2009). *Differentiation made simple: Timesaving tools for teachers.* Waco, TX: Prufrock Press. This practical guide offers tools for making differentiation doable.

⦿ Cash, R. M. (2011). *Advancing differentiation: Thinking and learning for the 21st century.* Minneapolis, MN: Free Spirit. This book and CD-ROM have examples useful for differentiating in classrooms.

⦿ Roberts, J. L., & Boggess, J. R. (2012). *Differentiating instruction with centers in the gifted classroom.* Waco, TX: Prufrock Press. This book provides an overview of differentiation and content-specific examples of differentiating for content, process, and product.

⦿ Sower, J., & Warner, L. (2011). *Differentiating instruction with centers in the inclusive classroom.* Waco, TX: Prufrock Press. This resource describes centers appropriate for primary classrooms.

⦿ Stanley, T. (2012). *Project-based learning for gifted students.* Waco, TX: Prufrock Press. Stanley gives an overview of project-based learning with ways to successfully implement it in the classroom.

⦿ Winebrenner, S. (1996). *Teaching kids with learning difficulties in the regular classroom.* Minneapolis, MN: Free Spirit. This is a great resource for effective differentiation strategies that work with students with learning difficulties.

⦿ Winebrenner, S. (2001). *Teaching gifted kids in the regular classroom.* Minneapolis, MN: Free Spirit. This resource includes an overview of differentiation with tips, strategies, and practical examples for how to make differentiation work.

Strategy 4: Graphic Organizers

Graphic organizers are visual tools created by teachers to help students organize and make sense of content. They may be used as advanced organizers, comprehension strategies, tools for activating background knowledge, formative assessments, or as a content review. The form and function of the graphic organizer is based on the content being taught and the type of thinking a teacher wants to encourage. For example, to preassess students' knowledge of content, a mind map might be used where students write down the concept and all connected ideas that they can remember. For compare and contrast, a T-chart is useful to help students organize similar attributes. For sequencing events in a story or steps of a problem, a flow chart graphic organizer is helpful.

Although all students can benefit from graphic organizers, it is also possible to use them to differentiate for student readiness or ability. Conklin (2010) suggested first choosing the standard, then articulating the skills or concepts to be learned, and then creating the graphic organizer that would work best for on-grade-level students. After that graphic organizer is created, she provided the following suggestions for adapting the graphic organizer for different learner needs:

- English Language Learners: Level the text in the examples on the graphic organizers, use a word bank with definitions, allow students to answer in pictures and/or words instead of writing sentences to summarize, label the titles and parts on the graphic organizers, let them verbally explain the graphic organizers, give individual or small-group instruction, provide recorded instructions or reminders using podcast software, etc.
- Below Grade Level: Provide a few examples already filled in on the graphic organizers, use an appropriately leveled word bank, let them write only one or two sentences to summarize the graphic organizer, label the titles and parts on the graphic organizers, provide lines to write on in the graphic organizers, simplify the directions, ask for fewer examples, etc.
- Above Grade Level: Increase complexity by adding another circle to the Venn diagram or another column to the T-chart, assign more ambiguous items to compare/contrast, give students a sophisticated word bank, let them work in homogenous groups, let them summarize the graphic organizers and then provide their evaluation of the situation, etc. (p. 71)

The following examples show ways to differentiate using a cause/effect chart and Venn diagram as graphic organizers. In the Being a Good Citizen lesson (see Figure 30), students are given one of three cause/effect charts based on their readiness. The first is a blank chart that allows students to fill in the causes and connect related effects; this is for students who are on-target for mastering the standard. The second provides some support to help students who are struggling or need additional scaffolds to prompt their thinking. The third chart requires those students who are ready for more complex thinking to complete the causes side of the chart, then also create both positive and negative effects and explain which is the most significant for each cause.

The graphic organizers in Figure 31 show how to differentiate using Venn diagrams in a fifth-grade classroom that is reading Rick Riordan's (2005) *The Lightning Thief*. The standard requires students to compare and contrast two or more characters, and there are three levels of Venn diagrams based on the level of complexity that students are ready to tackle. These could be given to students individually or in small groups.

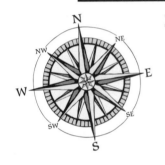

Survival Tips

- Struggling learners or English language learners may need more simplistic graphic organizers. The point of the visuals is to help students organize and process their thinking about content, so the chart itself should not be complicated and distracting. See more tips in Winebrenner's (1996) *Teaching Kids With Learning Difficulties in the Regular Classroom*.

- The cross-impact matrix in Cash's (2011) book would be an excellent graphic organizer for gifted students. This book contains samples of how to use the cross-impact matrix with the story of "The Three Little Pigs" and the Civil War.

Survival Tools

- Silver, H., Strong, R., & Perini, M. (2000). *Tools for promoting active, in-depth learning*. Ho-Ho-Kus, NJ: Thoughtful Education Press. This book describes strategies, including graphic organizers, to promote student thinking.

- Edhelper.com (http://edhelper.com/teachers/graphic_organizers. htm): This site houses examples of graphic organizers created by teachers.

- Education Place (http://www.eduplace.com/graphicorganizer): This website includes a variety of types of graphic organizers to use in any content area.

Lesson Title: Being a Good Citizen

Grade Levels: 3–4

Standards:

- *National Standards for Civics and Government*: What are important rights and responsibilities of citizens?
- *Reading*: Describe the relationship between a series of historical events, scientific ideas or concepts, or steps in technical procedures in a text, using language that pertains to time, sequence, and cause/effect.

Steps:

1. Give students one of the following three charts based on their readiness as they determine the causes and effects of citizenship.

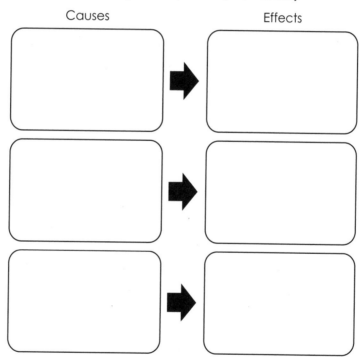

Cause and Effect Graphic Organizer
Citizenship: Home, School, Community

Causes   Effects

Figure 30. Being a Good Citizen lesson.

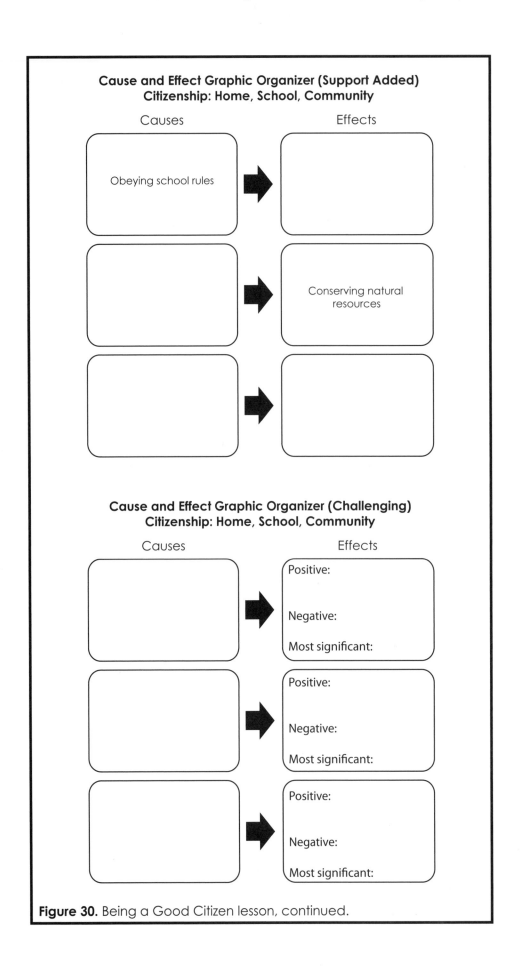

Figure 30. Being a Good Citizen lesson, continued.

Lesson Title: *The Lightning Thief*

Grade Level: 5

Standard:
- Compare and contrast two or more characters, settings, or events in a story or drama, drawing on specific details in the text (e.g., how characters interact).

Steps:
1. After students read *The Lightning Thief*, have them choose two or more characters in the book to study.
2. Provide students with one of the following Venn diagrams, based on the level of complexity they are ready for, to compare and contrast the characters they have chosen.

Venn Diagram Lesson: Two Ovals
The Lightning Thief (Percy Jackson and the Olympians)
by Rick Riordan
Compare and contrast the following characters.

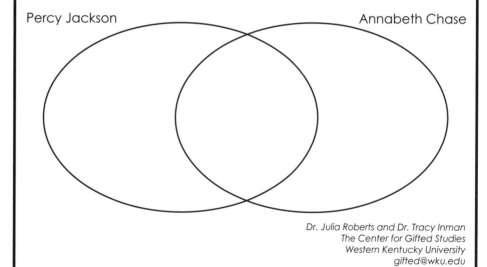

Percy Jackson   Annabeth Chase

Dr. Julia Roberts and Dr. Tracy Inman
The Center for Gifted Studies
Western Kentucky University
gifted@wku.edu

Figure 31. Venn diagram lesson.

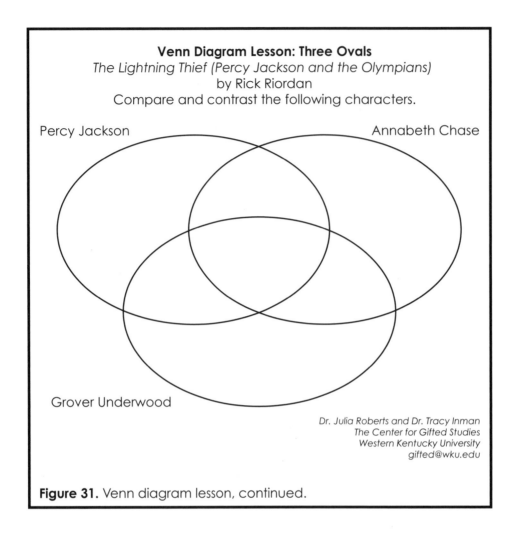

Venn Diagram Lesson: Three Ovals
The Lightning Thief (Percy Jackson and the Olympians)
by Rick Riordan
Compare and contrast the following characters.

Percy Jackson

Annabeth Chase

Grover Underwood

Dr. Julia Roberts and Dr. Tracy Inman
The Center for Gifted Studies
Western Kentucky University
gifted@wku.edu

Figure 31. Venn diagram lesson, continued.

Strategy 5: Leveled Questions

Using leveled questions is a way to adapt learning experiences to students' ability levels. Although it can be appropriate to level questions in a whole-group setting, in order to effectively match the strategy to the students' learning needs, leveled questions would best be used in either small groups or as assignments for students to answer individually. For instance, after examining preassessment or formative assessment results for a particular learning target, students could be placed into small groups based on whether they are on target with a standard, have already mastered the standard, or need extra support or practice with Bloom's remember and understand level tasks related to the standard.

Conklin (2010) suggested creating the on-target questions first, then adapting them for those who haven't mastered the target or those that are ready for more complex thinking. Using Bloom's cognitive levels for creating questions is a great place to start. Webb's (1999) Depth of Knowledge levels are also a great

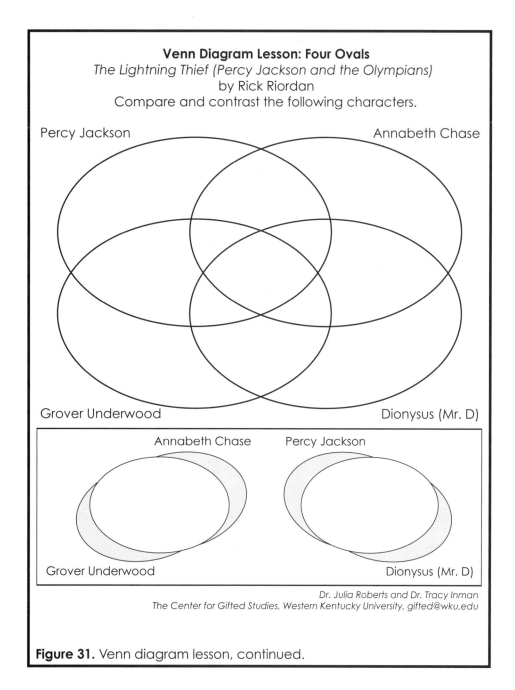

Figure 31. Venn diagram lesson, continued.

way to differentiate questions for cognitive complexity. Students who are struggling with the content may simply need more vocabulary support or examples. English language learners may need visuals or chunking the tasks into smaller parts to make it manageable.

Figure 32 shows questions that are leveled based on Bloom's taxonomy. After a formative assessment during a fourth-grade unit on life cycles, a teacher could either divide students into small groups or give these questions individually for students to work toward mastering the standard (i.e., differentiating for process). The triangle shape is for those that have mastered the basic remember and understand levels and are ready for application. Questions with the plus sign are for those who need more practice with remembering and understanding the content, and those with the heart are for students that are ready for the evaluate and create levels of Bloom. The teacher should cut these into strips and distribute to students.

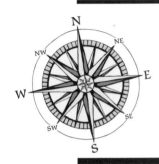

Survival Tips

- Carr's (2009) *Differentiation Made Simple: Timesaving Tools for Teachers* has a Tiered Question table that shows questions on the same content but on a continuum of difficulty. She also provides sample questions for each level of Bloom's taxonomy.

Survival Tools

- Depth of Knowledge (DOK) Levels Chart (http://dese.mo.gov/divimprove/sia/msip/DOK_Chart.pdf): This chart shows cognitive skills organized by DOK level. It is useful for creating leveled questions.

Concluding Comments

Each of these strategies can be used in a variety of ways based on varying the content, process, and/or product. The key to effective differentiation is to match the strategy to the content and the learner needs, interests, and readiness/abilities. When that happens, teachers can create a learning atmosphere where all students make continuous progress. That is the key to an effective differentiated classroom, one that Tomlinson and Imbeau (2010) described in "Yes, But . . . ," where the teacher has the power to change young lives every day by making the decisions that matter most.

Lesson Title: Life Cycles

Grade Level: 4

Standard:
- Investigate the life cycles of plants and animals to compare similarities and differences among organisms.

Steps:
1. When studying life cycles, cut the following sections into strips and provide them to students based on their readiness for the levels of Bloom's taxonomy.

• •

Answer the following questions about life cycles:

1. Choose two animals studied in class. Compare and contrast their life cycles in a T-chart.

2. Choose a new animal that we haven't studied. Based on the life cycle patterns you know, how would you classify this animal? Draw a picture of what you think its life cycle might be.

• •

Answer the following questions about life cycles:

1. Choose an animal studied in class. Draw a picture of its life cycle and label the steps.

2. Explain these concepts: complete and incomplete metamorphosis. Draw a visual example of each one.

• •

Answer the following questions about life cycles:

1. Design a cool or creepy new animal for a science fiction movie. Describe what its life cycle would be like.

2. Of all the examples studied in class (animals, birds, amphibians, reptiles, birds, etc.), which undergoes the most change or metamorphosis in its life cycle? Be able to give specific evidence to prove your argument.

Figure 32. Life Cycles lesson.

9 Using Technology to Differentiate

Contributed by Jennifer Smith and David Baxter

We need to prepare kids for their future, not our past.

—Daniel Pink

Key Question
- How do teachers use technology to enhance differentiation in their classrooms?

Teachers sometimes limit the primary functions of computers in the classroom to word processing, using search engines to find answers to questions, or reviewing skills via electronic worksheets and educational gaming sites. In the early years of technology adoption, that may have been adequate. Today, however, the Internet is more than a seemingly limitless source of information. In fact, it is increasingly a tool that requires interactions and inputs from the user. Technology is a powerful vehicle for creating and sharing quality work. As a result, the value of technology in the classroom has increased exponentially.

Now there is a wealth of rich and user-friendly resources available to classroom teachers—often at little or no cost. These Web 2.0 tools encourage creativity, facilitate communication, and aid in the development of authentic products. Web 2.0 revisions the Internet as a tool for social interaction, collaboration, creation, and community. Consequently, there are a number of benefits of technology in the classroom: technology promotes high levels of student engagement; children are learning to use the same tools as professionals; students can be creative and original in their thinking; real-world products can easily be saved and shared using cloud technology; and students have the ability to work at their own pace and their own level. Within the framework of continuous progress and instilling in students a lifelong capacity for learning, technology can be a tremendous resource for differentiation.

The Innovation Model/Philosophy

Of course, technology is best viewed as merely one tool in a teacher's toolbox. Technology supplements, but does not replace, hands-on learning experiences. Students still need to build, write, experiment, design, test, draw, read books and magazine articles, and experience field trips. Above all, students need opportunities to think deeply and discuss what they are learning.

Innovation can be understood as the synergy that exists when these varied processes interact. Although some would make bold distinctions between the contributions of the right brain and the left brain, it is too simplistic to say that scientists are logical and artists are creative, or mathematicians analyze while musicians intuit. An individual may demonstrate a strength in one area, but strict categorization becomes problematic. Leonardo da Vinci painted the *Mona Lisa*. Yet he was also a student of human anatomy, and his forward thinking envisioned a flying machine in the 15th century. Was he an artist, a scientist, or an engineer?

The Innovation Model (see Figure 33) proposes six key concepts, or portals, that are central to the innovative process: connect, inquire, create, analyze, enhance, and communicate. Each of these portals may be viewed as a doorway through which an individual might begin the process of innovation. It is a fluid, rather than linear, process, requiring a range of skills and, frequently, a team of collaborators. And it is a process that integrates skills from both sides of the brain.

Relate. Wonder. Imagine. Reflect. Respond. Share. Those are weighty ideas, and they are certainly not beyond the scope of the elementary curriculum. Technology is a valuable resource for introducing children to this exciting world of innovation. With individual students bringing unique skills, interests, and abilities to the classroom, differentiation is a necessity. But how does one manage a technology-rich learning environment with innovation at its heart?

Rigor and Relevance (Tool or Toy?)

The sheer volume of Web 2.0 programs and applications available for educational use can be overwhelming. Deciding which ones will be most effective can

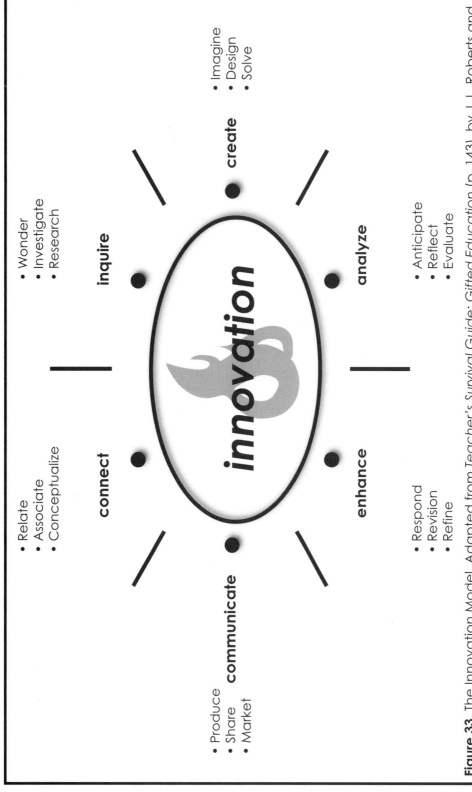

Figure 33. The Innovation Model. Adapted from *Teacher's Survival Guide: Gifted Education* (p. 143), by J. L. Roberts and J. R. Boggess, 2011, Waco, TX: Prufrock Press. Copyright 2011 by Prufrock Press. Reprinted with permission of David Baxter, Allison Bemiss, Julia Roberts, and Tracy Inman.

be a daunting and time-consuming task. With so many choices available, how do teachers best decide which tools will most effectively meet the needs of their students? Two important questions should guide these instructional decisions:

- Is this tool relevant to what my students must know, do, and understand?
- Does this tool provide an appropriate level of rigor to promote significant learning?

For many elementary children, of course, their main interaction with technology has been as a source of entertainment. Even at school, students often view time on the computer as a reward or as time to play games or surf "kid-friendly" websites. To be sure, real learning can occur in a game-based format. However, teachers must use sound judgment. Some online tools are quite engaging but may not lend themselves to legitimate instructional purposes. Teachers can address this distinction by simply being mindful of their own language. There is a marked difference between "working" on the computer and "playing" on the computer, and only the former is appropriate in the differentiated classroom.

Web 2.0 tools that meet the criteria for rigor and relevance typically fall into one of three categories. Some web tools are well suited for independent or self-directed learning. Differentiation strategies must address the needs of students across the learning spectrum, and the Internet offers numerous possibilities beyond shooting vowels and sums with virtual laser blasters. The Internet is also an excellent medium for students to share ideas, ask and answer questions, generate group products, and critique others' work. Collaboration tools enable students to communicate. Finally, technology-rich products have tremendous potential for assessing content knowledge and measuring growth. When used in conjunction with rubrics, products become a springboard for planning, problem solving, and creativity.

Web 2.0 for Independent Learning

If classrooms were entirely homogenous, there would be little need for differentiation. To the contrary, however, the contemporary classroom is more diverse than ever, and teachers must meet the individual needs of every student. One way to meet these needs is to provide individualized learning opportunities through technology. There is an unprecedented amount of rigorous and engaging educational content available online. Many of these resources are appropriate for creating differentiated learning experiences for students at various levels of academic readiness and across all content areas.

The teacher faces two challenges: selecting appropriate activities and efficiently communicating these learning opportunities to students. Whether the goal is intervention, acceleration, or simply a response to student interest, a quality activity should engage the mind with an appropriate level of challenge.

Unlike games that require only recall and rote memorization, rigorous educational activities require a degree of problem solving. Some websites have indexed many of these activities in one convenient location.

Crickweb (http://www.crickweb.co.uk) and nrich (http://www.nrich.maths.org), both free online resources from the United Kingdom, have content arranged by developmental level and subject area. The Oswego City School District (http://resources.oswego.org/games) in Oswego, NY, offers an array of challenging mathematics activities. Students will enjoy learning about angles with "Banana Hunt" and telling time with "Stop the Clock." Other free mathematics resources include the National Library of Virtual Manipulatives (http://nlvm.usu.edu) from Utah State University and Illuminations (http://illuminations.nctm.org) developed by the National Council of Teachers of Mathematics. Once again, both sites are searchable by specific grade level.

With tens of thousands of free resources arranged by grade level, subject area, and media type, PBS LearningMedia™ (http://www.pbslearningmedia.org) is a treasure trove of information. Audio and video clips, images, documents, and interactives are linked to various state and national standards for subjects ranging from language arts and social studies to science and mathematics. Another worthwhile resource is BrainPOP (http://www.brainpop.com), which features short, animated videos covering a plethora of topics. Conveniently searchable by grade level, subject area, and state standards, BrainPOP is a place for learning about polynomials, Maya Angelou, and the International Space Station. Primary teachers should also check out BrainPOP Jr. (http://www.brainpopjr.com), which is geared toward students in grades K–3.

Networking with colleagues and attending technology-specific professional development can have a profound impact on one's knowledge of existing resources. Some educators even enjoy sharing and learning new ideas through social media such as Twitter and Pinterest. The number of available options is increasing daily; the key is to always have a clear purpose in mind before putting technology in the hands of your students.

Teachers can also utilize technology to guide students to the intended resource. One cannot simply direct students to a website with dozens of resources and expect them to select something appropriate. For example, the website of Ambleside Primary School in Nottingham, England, features a Learning Zone with several quality mathematics activities. Students, however, would soon find their way to Ambleside Arcade, which has no educational merit whatsoever. The teacher must connect the student with the resource in a very deliberate way.

Dictating a complicated URL to a roomful of students is rather inefficient. Symbaloo (http://www.symbaloo.com) is a free online bookmarking tool that allows users to bookmark a specific URL using a graphic icon. This is an excellent point of entry for all students. The Symbaloo account can link to multiple websites, enabling even young children or others with limited English proficiency to navigate directly to sites the teacher selects. Equally powerful, though less visually appealing, is Diigo (http://www.diigo.com), another online bookmarking tool. Like Symbaloo, Diigo creates "virtual" bookmarks, meaning they can be accessed from any location using any device with an Internet connection. These are but two examples. Regardless of the method selected, the goal is to swiftly connect students with quality content. And that typically does not happen when students are searching on Google and Yahoo! or transcribing a lengthy URL from the whiteboard.

Glogster (http://edu.glogster.com; see Figure 34) deserves special mention. Glogster is a wonderful organization and presentation tool that allows the user to embed text, images, links, and videos directly into a digital poster. Many teachers have used this to great effect to organize online materials for a lesson or unit. The result is a user-friendly interface with tremendous visual appeal. And, rather than saving a Glog to the user's hard drive, the actual product is stored on the cloud. Teachers can easily create a Glog at home, then access and edit it at school. Intermediate students can certainly use Glogster to demonstrate their own learning. This is an ideal way for teachers to assess using authentic products.

Students of all ages feel empowered when teachers ask them what they want to learn, how they want to learn it, and how they prefer to show what they know. Teachers can use Google Docs (http://docs.google.com) to effortlessly synthesize this information from online forms. Once the form is created (see Figure 35), students can access the survey from any computer. The program automatically saves all student data to a spreadsheet in real time, giving the teacher instant access to the results. This information is essential for managing independent study projects or creating cluster groups with similar academic interests and learning styles.

Finally, although still a relatively new idea, the concept of the "flipped classroom" is generating a great deal of interest across the educational community. In a flipped classroom, students do not practice newly acquired skills as homework. Rather, students practice at school with the teacher available to coach, guide, and mentor them. In this model, instruction is delivered at home via podcast, video, or other online resource. Teachers can, of course, create their own online content. However, one very popular resource for the flipped classroom is Khan Academy (http://www.khanacademy.org). The brainchild of founder Salman Khan, an alumnus of both Harvard and MIT, Khan Academy boasts a free library of thousands of instructional videos, along with teacher tools for tracking student progress. A great addition to the toolbox of educators looking to differentiate, these videos are suitable for students across the learning spectrum.

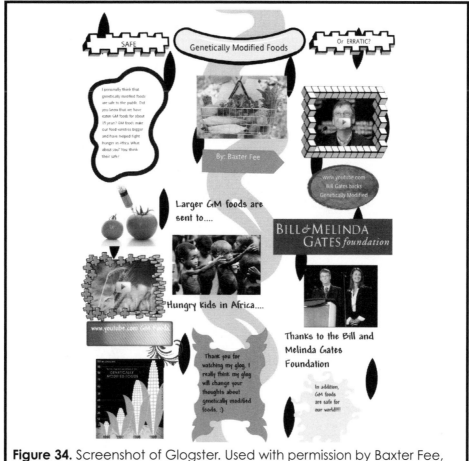

Figure 34. Screenshot of Glogster. Used with permission by Baxter Fee, Project GEMS Academy.

Collaboration Tools

Most great learning happens in groups. Collaboration is the stuff of growth.

—Sir Ken Robinson

When a teacher is initially asked to think about the term *differentiation*, the first image that may come to mind is of every student in the classroom working independently on his or her own individual assignments and projects. For other teachers, they may picture students grouped together at various tables in clusters based on their levels of academic readiness. But another facet of differentiation is to give students the freedom to think beyond the limitations of responding to teacher-generated questions or prompts about given topics. Differentiation encompasses the entire process of providing each student with the opportunity to think creatively and to innovate, to seek answers to his own

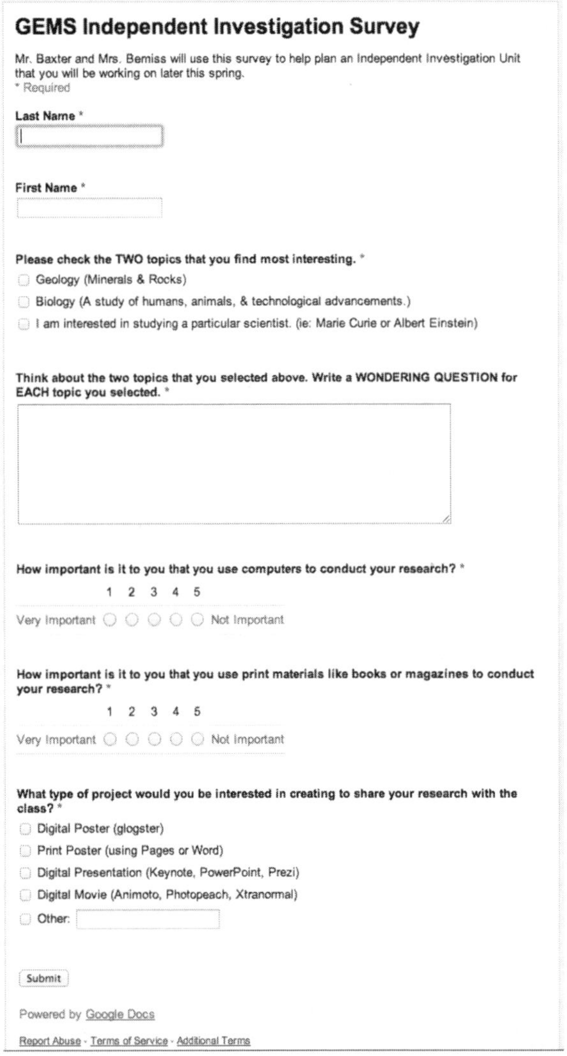

GEMS Independent Investigation Survey

Mr. Baxter and Mrs. Bemiss will use this survey to help plan an Independent Investigation Unit that you will be working on later this spring.
* Required

Last Name *

First Name *

Please check the TWO topics that you find most interesting. *
- Geology (Minerals & Rocks)
- Biology (A study of humans, animals, & technological advancements.)
- I am interested in studying a particular scientist. (ie: Marie Curie or Albert Einstein)

Think about the two topics that you selected above. Write a WONDERING QUESTION for EACH topic you selected. *

How important is it to you that you use computers to conduct your research? *

      1 2 3 4 5

Very Important ◯ ◯ ◯ ◯ ◯ Not Important

How important is it to you that you use print materials like books or magazines to conduct your research? *

      1 2 3 4 5

Very Important ◯ ◯ ◯ ◯ ◯ Not Important

What type of project would you be interested in creating to share your research with the class? *
- Digital Poster (glogster)
- Print Poster (using Pages or Word)
- Digital Presentation (Keynote, PowerPoint, Prezi)
- Digital Movie (Animoto, Photopeach, Xtranormal)
- Other:

Submit

Powered by Google Docs

Report Abuse · Terms of Service · Additional Terms

Figure 35. Google Docs example.

questions, and to delve into topics using her own unique perspectives, learning styles, and strengths.

In an educational environment of high-stakes testing focused on students' individual test scores, it is easy to lose sight of the power of collaboration in the classroom. Despite exhaustive research confirming the effectiveness of social learning, it can be difficult to trust that these experiences will translate to proficient scores on standardized assessments. Of course it is important for every student to know and understand core content material, but thinking *for* yourself is not necessarily the same as thinking *by* yourself. Although the term *collective intelligence* is a relatively new entry into the educational lexicon, the idea behind it is not; the adage "the whole is greater than the sum of its parts" originated from Aristotle in reference to the power of group synergy. Great things happen when every student brings his or her own intellectual strengths to the table.

In Robinson's (2011) book, *Out of Our Minds: Learning to Be Creative*, he discusses the important role of collaboration in the creative process:

> The popular image of creativity is of the lone genius swimming heroically against an oppressive tide of convention pursuing ideas that no one has had before. . . . But the idea of the lone genius can be misleading. Original ideas may emanate from the creative inspiration of individual minds, but they do not emerge in a cultural vacuum. . . . Individual creativity is almost always stimulated by the work, ideas and achievements of other people. (p. 197)

One of the key tenets of the "revisioning" of Web 2.0 is recognizing the power of online technology to enhance student learning through collaboration with their peers. Using technology as a communication and collaboration tool, students are no longer limited to whole-class or small-group discussions, turn-and-talks, or raising their hand to speak and share their ideas publicly. So often, children who are more reserved during class discussions have much to contribute that remains unsaid, robbing the entire classroom community of their valuable and unique insights. Online collaboration tools provide a democratic forum for every student to write about their thoughts, discuss opinions, share links, and ask questions. Real-time virtual conversations act as natural extensions of class discussions and mini-lessons. The teacher can continue to act as a facilitator of the learning environment, but students can now interact in a more spontaneous and organic fashion by using Web 2.0 tools to harness the power of social learning.

There are multiple easy-to-use Web 2.0 collaboration tools available on the Internet for free. These applications can be set up as "public" or "private," giving the teacher full control of who can view and enter the forum. One popular educational tool is Edmodo (http://www.edmodo.com), a secure platform with a user interface similar to Facebook and the basic functionality of Blackboard, which is frequently used for college-level online coursework. Each student has an individual username and password and is provided with a group code to join discussion boards set up by the teacher. The teacher can share content, links, and other materials with students; create assignments; and moderate student discussions. There is no individual peer-to-peer interaction. Edmodo is an excellent way for students to network on collaborative research projects, debate topics, and share knowledge with their peers. This tool is better suited for students in the intermediate grades.

Lino (http://www.linoit.com) is a highly visual application that lets students post their thoughts on an online pinboard. Students can create their own customizable virtual sticky notes and "stick" them to the screen to share with the class. This serves essentially the same function as students responding to a teacher prompt on real sticky notes and then collating them on anchor charts. Pinboards can be saved indefinitely, and one avoids the inconvenience of notes being shed all over the classroom floor at the end of the day. Students don't have to crowd around an easel to try to see their classmates' input—it's fully visible right in front of them on their computer screen. Figure 36 provides a visual image of how Edmodo and Lino can be used in a classroom.

Another interesting and highly engaging collaboration tool is SpiderScribe (http://www.spiderscribe.com), an online interactive concept-mapping tool. Students can collaboratively mind-map and brainstorm ideas on a virtual graphic organizer that they create together. This is also an excellent platform for students to engage in nonlinear written conversations and debates. SpiderScribe is simple to learn and easy to use, and students love when a classmate "connects" a related response to one of their thought bubbles. As with Lino and Edmodo, the teacher acts as the moderator and is able to remove any off-topic student posts.

Although not used for written collaboration, another Web 2.0 tool that bears mentioning is Skype (http://www.skype.com). Skype is a free online face-to-face video chat application that operates in real time. Using a webcam, students can interact with other students, teachers, and experts across the globe. Skype is a fantastic way for students to interview authors, scientists, or other professionals without having to arrange for a cost-prohibitive speaker or field trip. There are multiple resources available online to help teachers find other classrooms to Skype with from around the world.

Products as Assessments

How does a teacher know if students understand the assigned content? By giving a written cumulative test, of course! That may have been the correct answer years ago, but today's teachers understand that assessment occurs during all stages of the learning process: preassessments given to find out what students already know, formative assessments to gauge learning throughout the unit, and summative assessments at the end to see what knowledge has been retained. But these certainly don't all have to take the form of a test or quiz, as student-generated products are another excellent way to assess what students can do, know, and understand.

Web 2.0 tools offer a wealth of possibilities for students to design products to share with real-world audiences, giving tangible evidence of their depth and breadth of understanding of a given topic. Using technology to create digital presentations, slideshows, movies, podcasts, and animated shorts engages

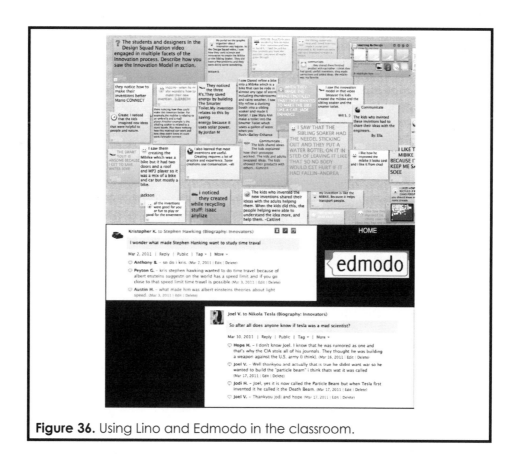

Figure 36. Using Lino and Edmodo in the classroom.

students in active learning while also providing the teacher a product for assessment. Additionally, working with Web 2.0 tools gives students the autonomy to work at their own pace, to learn how to use the same or similar computer applications as those used by professionals, and to communicate their thoughts and ideas in an interactive format. Whether alone or in a group, students are constantly problem solving as they work to craft a substantive, polished presentation. Opportunities for virtual and real-world collaboration abound.

In certain instances, working with technology can remove the obstacles some children face when asked to complete a handcrafted project such as a poster, trifold display, or brochure. There is nothing inherently wrong with asking students to create these types of products for a class assignment. However, children with poor handwriting, those with less-than-stellar drawing skills, and others who struggle with organizing visual layouts may find themselves penalized due to aesthetic issues. The rubric for a digital presentation can reflect high standards for presentation while still removing some of the potentially hidden barriers to performance.

Technology can function as a scaffold for students to learn the elements of a well-designed product. Online presentation tools such as Prezi (http://www.prezi.com) and offline products like Microsoft's PowerPoint and Apple's

Keynote offer preset themes and layouts for users to choose from. (Google Docs, mentioned previously, offers free web-based document, presentation, and spreadsheet programs that work with any computer platform.) Students are not limited to using these templates, but they do provide a solid basis to help create a polished-looking product. As they design their products, students begin to make connections about choosing fonts, colors, and layouts that will complement and enhance the tone of their presentation. Meanwhile, multiple rounds of editing and revising are expected, making that a natural and acceptable part of the production process.

One objection frequently heard regarding students using technology for projects is that not all students have equal access to computers and other devices at home. Therefore, giving digital assignments may put some students at a disadvantage. Fundamentally, however, this is no different than asking students with limited resources to produce a project such as a brochure, diorama, poster, or model to be compared to those of their classmates. One way around this issue is to simply allow time during the instructional day for students to work on their projects instead of making them take-home endeavors. Most public libraries also offer free Internet access to their patrons. Keeping technology out of the hands of the students who already have little access to it for economic reasons does not make sense in the big picture.

One of the most important aspects of project-based learning is having students present their digital products to their classmates. Products are created for an authentic audience, not just for the teacher. This experience is good for building oral communication skills, it allows other students to analyze the presentation and give feedback, and it gives children a chance to see what kind of work their peers are doing. Presenting their work and getting positive feedback helps students build confidence, and constructive criticism often motivates them to sit down and immediately start making improvements to enhance their work.

Along with using Glogster and Prezi (both discussed previously) as presentation tools, teachers might want to consider PhotoPeach (http://www.photopeach.com), GoAnimate (http://www.goanimate4schools.com), or Xtranormal (http://www.xtranormal.com/edu). PhotoPeach allows users to generate photo slideshows accompanied by music and text. This makes students' writing purposeful. They also enjoy selecting music that complements the theme or topic of their presentation. A student presentation on Jane Goodall, for example, could feature a soundtrack that reflects the music of east Africa. GoAnimate and Xtranormal, both of which are paid options, are tools for creating short animated clips. Students can use storyboards for planning and sequencing, and, as with PhotoPeach, creating the narration gives their writing real purpose.

Even the youngest students will enjoy working with Storybird (http://www.storybird.com). Storybird has a tremendous gallery of beautiful artwork by professional artists. Students can sequence these images to create their own stories, to which they provide the narration. It is not uncommon to introduce a tool like Storybird at school, only to find out that some students go home and spend hours creating their own Storybirds for fun!

Rubrics

In order for anyone to create a successful product, it is only fair for him to know what a quality product might look like. Students should always have a rubric to guide their work, from the planning phase through final revisions. Premade rubrics are widely available, but the best rubrics are often the result of student input. Through guided discussion, students can identify the characteristics that define quality work.

Because learning is the ultimate goal for all students, it is important for the rubric to reflect content knowledge. Of course, students must also be aware of the various elements of a professional presentation (e.g., aesthetics, organization), but the meat of the rubric should address student thinking. Are they asking important questions? Are they able to make key connections? Are they thinking analytically? The rubric is also a useful touchstone for peer review. When a student thinks his work is complete, a classmate can evaluate his product against the rubric and offer suggestions for ways to refine and enhance the presentation. Even analysis and reflection should be a collaborative effort. Figure 37 provides a sample rubric for a digital presentation.

Practical Matters: Digital Citizenship and Management of Technology

Students as young as kindergarten have probably already used technology extensively outside of the school setting. There are countless stories of students quickly fixing issues with computers, peripherals, and network settings that have caused adults many hours of frustration. Referring to the fact that technology has been an integral part of their lives since birth, Prensky (2001) coined the term *digital natives* to describe the present generation. Technology is not a new concept for them. It is considered a normal, functional component of their everyday lives, not simply a novelty or sideline activity. Still, it is unreasonable to assume that students will have a firm grasp of safety and ethics, or that they will never feel anxiety when working with a tool that's new for them.

Teaching students digital citizenship and developing a sensible management plan will help to ensure the effective use of technology in the classroom. It is essential to establish and communicate clear expectations regarding the appropriate use of technology, especially when students will be working online. Even though most students are very motivated to use computers and find them highly engaging, they will not know what parameters the teacher has in mind

Name: _____

Method: _____

Score: _____

How Does Your Garden Grow?

☐ Glog   ☐ PhotoPeach   ☐ GoAnimate

Innovation Concept	Criteria	Points	Notes
Connect	How does this method of gardening reflect the three R's: reduce, reuse, recycle?	10	
Inquire	What special knowledge, materials, or procedures are necessary for this method of gardening?	10	
Create	Does the presentation reflect professional-level work (i.e., clarity, organization, use of time, etc.)?	5	
Analyze	Does this method of gardening present any special benefits or obstacles?	10	
Enhance	How could you refine this method of gardening for application in your own home or school?	10	
Communicate	Are you communicating with your peers in appropriate ways (i.e., focused presentation, adequate voice level, etc.)?	5	

Figure 37. Digital presentation rubric.

or what is considered productive use of their time without some frontloading, preteaching, and guidance.

Digital Citizenship

One of the first concepts that students need to internalize is the idea of digital citizenship. Digital citizenship is a broad term that covers, but is not limited to, issues of Internet safety, etiquette, and an understanding of intellectual property and creative rights for online content and images. District release forms granting students Internet access at school do not negate the importance of clear-cut classroom-level policies and expectations for students' computer usage.

Students often respond well to discussions of digital citizenship that are presented or facilitated by their peers. Many elementary schools have a Student Technology Leadership Program (STLP) geared toward intermediate students. It is likely that most STLP groups will have access to digital citizenship presentations that they can share with students in other grade levels. Middle and high school students may even be available to share digital citizenship presentations with the entire elementary student body.

Online Etiquette

If students will be collaborating through Lino, Edmodo, or other similar forums, it is imperative that they grasp the principles of online etiquette. It needs to be made clear that bullying or gossiping will not be tolerated and making derogatory comments about other students, their ideas, or projects is unacceptable. A class discussion about how to respectfully disagree and offer constructive criticism is imperative, and an anchor chart with guidelines about how to do so should be posted in a highly visible place in the classroom. Online communications between students should be on topic and task-oriented. Remind students that "shout-outs" to friends and inside jokes aren't appropriate in an educational setting, as they can create an unwelcoming environment for students who do not feel socially included.

Internet Safety

Internet safety is another critical topic for teachers, parents, and school administrators. Although most school districts have Internet filters in place to try to block inappropriate and questionable content, it is virtually impossible to find everything that should be blocked! Occasionally, seemingly innocuous searches can turn up completely unrelated websites. There are several different tactics that teachers can employ to reduce the potential for students to access inappropriate content from school.

- Students should be instructed *never* to give out any personal information online such as their full name, address, or phone number.
- Students should only be allowed on secure forums that are administrated by their teacher and limited to users from within their school or classroom.
- Prohibit students from registering for memberships to websites, gaming sites, or forums or downloading applications while at school.
- Always empower students to inform adults of any questionable content they may find while online. Most students naturally worry about getting in trouble if they are on an inappropriate site. Reassure them that it is better to say something to their teacher than to try to hide it.
- If necessary, a quick check of the browser's "History" tool can give a teacher some background on how a student may have ended up on a particular website.
- Do not allow students to access YouTube to search for video content. A website called SchoolTube (http://www.schooltube.com) is a much safer choice for educational and kid-friendly content.

Creative Rights and Intellectual Property

One of the gray areas for many teachers and students when working with Web 2.0 tools is determining when information found online is considered public domain as opposed to someone else's intellectual property. Many students erroneously believe that it is fine to cut and paste information as it is found online directly into their own work. This is no more acceptable than copying a passage verbatim directly from a book and trying to pass it off as one's own! Be sure to give students guidance on how to properly cite their sources whenever they are involved in online research.

Another issue that can arise is choosing images or music for a student project. Some services, such as PhotoPeach, offer proprietary selections of music that students are free to use when creating a photo slideshow on their site. However, anything that is copyrighted cannot be integrated into a student project without permission of the owner of the creative rights. Luckily, sites for copyright-free clip art and photographic images are plentiful. Take the time to bookmark a few of these sites for student use. Two useful sites for students to find public domain images are Pics4Learning (http://www.pics4learning.com) and Classroom Clipart (http://www.classroomclipart.com).

Management of Technology

One of the biggest challenges for many classroom teachers is creating adequate blocks of time for students to access technology. For some, this difficulty is due to daily scheduling constraints; for others, it may be the seemingly inadequate number of computers available for student use. Vexing as they are at times, these obstacles can be overcome to provide meaningful opportunities for students to use technology. Of course, this may require teachers to draw from their reserve of ingenuity and flexibility!

Management strategies. Although student access to computers on a 1:1 ratio is certainly an ideal situation, it is still the exception to the rule in most school districts. That said, more and more schools are moving in this direction for the future. Generally speaking, most elementary schools currently have enough computers in a lab setting and/or mobile laptops carts for use by at least one full homeroom of students at the same time. Some schools may also have a small number of desktop computers available for student use within each classroom. Regardless of the availability of technology, it is important for teachers to incorporate a few helpful management strategies so students can maximize the productivity of their computer time.

- Have a precise plan for what students are supposed to be doing while online and clearly communicate those expectations to students.
- Provide students graphic organizers to scaffold the research process—what information do they need to be looking for?
- Have students create pencil-and-paper storyboards to plan out presentations before working on digital products.
- Make posters or "cheat sheets" available that include step-by-step instructions and visual cues on how to save and retrieve student files.
- Students tend to need longer periods of uninterrupted time for research and for creating digital products. Such activities are good options for longer blocks of time in the computer lab.
- Many learning games and applications are well suited for use as self-directed activities during centers, as a 10–15-minute window is frequently adequate time for students to complete the activity.
- Use Web 2.0 tools such as Glogster, Symbaloo, or Diigo to organize direct links to the specific online applications students need to be using.
- Keep a spreadsheet handy of all student login and password information.

Maximizing student access to technology. Finding ways to maximize student access to technology often involves deliberate planning and creative scheduling by the teacher. Although there is no magic solution for situations when devices may simply be in short supply, this cannot be viewed as an excuse to avoid trying to integrate technology at all. Here are a few different ways to work smart when trying to secure time for students to work with technology:

- When students will be working on long-term projects, make sure to schedule a series of blocks of time for the computer lab or laptop cart well ahead of time.

- Use headphone splitters for pairs of students or small groups sharing a single computer or iPad to cut down on noise and distractions.
- Schedule student computer time in rotation during centers.
- Allow students who have a compacted curriculum to work independently with online learning tools while other students work as a group with the teacher.
- Plan collaborative lessons with computer teachers, library media specialists, and resource teachers that integrate technology.
- Coordinate schedules with colleagues to allow students who are working independently to quietly use desktop computers that are available in other classrooms.

Concluding Comments

The integration of technology into the elementary school classroom opens up a whole new world of opportunity for students to learn, create, and innovate. An abundance of excellent Web 2.0 tools exist to help teachers develop rigorous and relevant differentiated learning experiences to meet the individualized needs of every student. In a world moving at a constant and exponential rate of change, today's teachers are tasked with preparing students for careers that don't even exist yet. Although content skills are important, teaching children to ask questions and seek answers, collaborate productively with others, persevere when presented with challenges, and strive for continual improvement are lessons that will carry on throughout each child's journey as a lifelong learner.

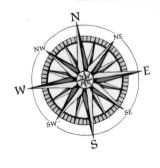

Survival Tips

- Don't limit yourself—or your students—by only using tools you've mastered. Obviously, you want to avoid a management nightmare. On the other hand, it is okay for students to struggle a bit when learning how to use a new tool. Challenge builds perseverance. And you may find that the most unlikely students quickly become "experts," helping their classmates (and teachers!) master the latest technology.

- Learn from your colleagues: Ask other teachers which Web 2.0 tools they are using; follow educational Twitter feeds, blogs, and Pinterest sites; and attend technology-specific professional development sessions.

- To keep from getting overwhelmed, choose just one or two new applications that you really want to learn.

Working with the applications for only 10–20 minutes a day will make you a pro in a matter of weeks!

- Does the web tool have a special account option for educators? Is the educator option more secure? Is it free?

- Use the same e-mail address, login, and password for all of your accounts. Create a free e-mail account for your class to use as a shared username (e.g., ourclass123@ gmail.com).

- Remember, technology products make excellent summative assessments!

Survival Tools

- BrainPOP (http://www.brainpop.com): This is a wonderful educational site with short, fun, but highly informative animated movies explaining topics from across the K–12 core content. It includes student quizzes and related activities for each topic. There is also a BrainPOP Jr. site (http://www.brainpopjr.com), which is specifically for K–3 students. Some content can be accessed for free, but access to the full site is subscription-based.

- Cool Tools for Schools (http://cooltoolsforschools.wikispaces.com): This is an awarding-winning wiki with very extensive listings and links for online educational resources organized by type (i.e., mapping tools, research tools, etc.).

- Diigo (http://www.diigo.com): This is a Web 2.0 tool that allows users to quickly and easily bookmark sites to a shared online library. Links can be organized into lists and tagged for easy retrieval.

- Edmodo (http://www.edmodo.com): This is a secure online social media forum based on a Facebook-like interface for teachers and students to collaborate, communicate, host discussions, share content, and create and follow assignments.

- Glogster (http://www.edu.glogster.com): This is a simple-to-use Web 2.0 tool for creating interactive poster-style web pages. Students can embed text, images, video content, animations, and links.

- The Khan Academy (http://www.khanacademy.org): This is a free site with more than 3,000 educational tutorial videos, interactive challenges, and assessments for self-directed learning for students. There is also a real-time class report function that teachers can set up free of charge to manage students' online learning.

- Lino (http://www.linoit.com): This is a free online sticky-note message board. It's a fun way to let students post feedback and comments to an assigned question or prompt.

- PBS LearningMedia™ (http://www.pbslearningmedia.org): This is a collection of more than 16,000 classroom-ready digital resources including videos and interactives, audio, photos, and in-depth lesson plans that are all available free for educators. Materials can be searched by grade level, content area, and media type.

- PhotoPeach (http://www.photopeach.com): This is a Web 2.0 tool that allows students to easily create professional-looking slideshow presentations by uploading photos and images, adding captions, and choosing from a selection of copyright free music.

- Pics4Learning (http://www.pics4learning.com) and Classroom Clipart (http://classroomclipart.com): These are both useful sites for students to find public domain images.

- Poisson Rouge (French for "red fish"; http://www.poissonrouge.com): This website consists of interactive environments designed by linguists, graphic artists, musicians, and educational psychologists for children of all ages. It contains neither text nor instructions, but carefully designed visual environments and soundscapes for the user to explore. This amazing site truly has to be experienced to be understood!

- Prezi (http://www.prezi.com): This is a "zooming" presentation tool that adds depth and visual interest. It can be navigated in a nonlinear progression.

- SchoolTube (http://www.schooltube.com): This is a safe alternative to YouTube for viewing and sharing educational video content.

- SpiderScribe (http://www.spiderscribe.com): This is an online mind-mapping and brainstorming tool. Students can organize their ideas by connecting notes and files in free-form maps and then collaborate and share those maps online. It is also a great tool for "silent" student discussions and debates.

- Storybird (http://www.storybird.com): This is a Web 2.0 site loaded with stunning illustrations designed to stimulate students' imaginations and spark creative writing. It's an excellent tool for English language learners, emerging readers, and aspiring authors at any age level.

- Symbaloo (http://www.symbaloo.com): This is an online tool that helps teachers create a visual command center, using symbols instead of words to link to bookmarked sites for student use. This is a valuable tool for teachers with English language learners and emergent readers in their classrooms.

10 Managing a Differentiated Classroom

A teacher who has the best intentions, dynamic curriculum, and plans for differentiation cannot—and will not—move forward unless that teacher is at ease with translating the ideas into classroom practice.

—Carol A. Tomlinson and Marcia Imbeau

Key Question

- How do teachers effectively manage a differentiated classroom?

Establishing and practicing procedures and routines are essential in order to make differentiation manageable in the classroom. Classroom culture that supports diversity and challenge sets the proper background for differentiated learning experiences. The Effective Differentiation Model (see Chapter 2) features differentiated content, process, and products on a background of classroom climate. Without a classroom climate to support and encourage continuous progress and lifelong learning, efforts to differentiate will be short lived. This chapter addresses many of the questions educators have concerning the daily practices that make differentiation doable.

Questions and Answers

How Might a Differentiated Class Look and Sound Different From a Traditional Class?

A differentiated classroom may trade straight rows of desks for tables that can be used for myriad purposes or for desks that can be configured and reconfigured based on need. Perhaps beanbag chairs are nestled in a reading corner near a low bookshelf, easily accessible to readers. Instead of the teacher's desk being placed front and center, it may be tucked away in a corner, allowing more space. Differentiating often involves hands-on, minds-on learning, so a differentiated classroom will have a supply area complete with resources. Donning the walls will be charts of table set-ups so that children can easily prepare the classroom for whatever kind of learning is taking place. These charts can show how to put desks and chairs together if working in pairs, in triads, in groups of five children, or for whole-group activities. Children will know where to put their own chair for any of these arrangements once the arrangement is announced. Reminders of rules and procedures will also be scattered to help ensure smooth transitions and an organized schedule.

How Do I Organize Materials and Resources?

Differentiated classrooms are not only minds-on, but hands-on as well. Hands-on means a lot of stuff—such as materials to create products that demonstrate learning and furniture and supplies in areas of the classroom indicative of the content studied there (e.g., bean bags in the reading area and a fish tank in the science section). Organization is key. For example, bins and baskets are probably needed in each area of the classroom to hold math manipulatives, crayons, and all of the supplies needed for learning that content. Labels on the bins remind students where to get what they need and where to return things when they are finished. A filing cabinet holding generic product rubrics encourages students to develop a wide variety of quality products.

Color-coding can be especially effective. For example, yellow may be associated with all thing math related. Yellow-colored bins can hold the tangrams and dice. A yellow poster on the wall can remind students of procedures related to math groups. Math resources for various ability levels could be lined up on the yellow shelf of the bookcase. Students could keep the math assignments they are working on in a yellow folder and put the completed ones in a yellow basket on the teacher's desk. The goal is optimum organization so that time—such a precious commodity in the classroom—is devoted to instruction and learning, not shuffling papers or searching for glue sticks.

What Are Different Grouping Possibilities?

Some forms of grouping occur before the school year begins. Classes that are grouped by readiness or ability are intended to match students to content level, and such grouping must be in place as the school starts for the year. For example, one fifth-grade math class may be working above grade level (i.e., sixth-grade math or prealgebra), while another works at grade level, and yet another is planned to help students reach grade level. Of course, differentiation and various groupings need to occur within the classes, but students with roughly the same abilities or experiences with the content are placed in the appropriate classes at the beginning of the school year. Another grouping technique that takes place before the year begins is cluster grouping. Cluster grouping takes five to eight students who are advanced or have high ability in one area and places them together in the same class with the same teacher for that subject. The teacher should ideally be trained in gifted education, a specialist in differentiation, and a content expert. Experience suggests that the teacher is much more likely to differentiate for a small group than he would be for one or two students. Not only do these children grow cognitively, but they also grow socially and emotionally because they are grouped at least for part of the day with children who are like them—they have a peer group. New leaders also tend to rise. These two forms of grouping are typically administrative decisions, so school leaders need to know the value in grouping children before school begins for the year.

Whether or not the class is heterogeneously grouped before the school year starts, the educator has the power to group and regroup children in their classroom. Educators, for example, could create cooperative learning groups. Although there is an educational objective and all groups are working toward that goal, the primary emphasis is on developing social and communication skills. Often these groups are heterogeneous and, consequently, the task may not be equally challenging for all children in the class. A note of caution: In cooperative learning groups, gifted children should be grouped together instead of being sprinkled among the other groups. Each group needs to have a task that is equally challenging to members of the cooperative group.

Children may be grouped for instructional or noninstructional purposes throughout the school year. For example, children may be grouped by self-selection in order to boost motivation or they may be randomly assigned to a group in order to have more children get to know each other. Either way, the groups will have the same assignment, so no differentiation of instruction takes place—the groups are based on noninstructional reasoning. In order to group for instructional purposes, groups of children will have different learning experiences based on the reason for the grouping. Grouping by interests, multiple intelligences, learning modalities, or readiness levels dictate the assignments. Content, process, or product is matched to interest, need, or ability, so differentiation occurs. Ideally children will be flexibly grouped where the educator varies grouping intent (e.g., pairing children according to learning modality for one unit, then by readiness for another learning experience). The key, of course, is appropriate placement to ensure that learning is ongoing as continuous progress and lifelong learning are goals of school and of a differentiated classroom.

When Is Grouping Appropriate?

In most schools, children are grouped into grade-level classes by the randomness of their birthdays. So in many classrooms grouping is being done by age alone—not for any of the numerous defensible ways to group discussed in the last question. Flexible grouping within the class is always appropriate if it is for instructional purposes. Educators must consider the content to be taught. Some concepts require whole-group instruction and individual practice. Others lend themselves more to grouping based on interests, readiness, or learning profiles. Oftentimes the preassessment can guide the structure. For example, if the preassessment indicates that the lesson's essential concepts are new to the entire class, then direct instruction may be the better choice.

When Do Groups Need to Change?

Formative assessment results keep the teacher well informed about student progress toward learning targets. It is important for the teacher to document learning progress with written records (technology provides the means for record keeping with an iPad or other device). As one child or several children demonstrate that they have reached a point that they need added challenge or more support, then that is the time to change the assignments. This may also mean moving groups or it may mean that it is time to reassess what learning experiences will be more likely to facilitate continuous progress.

How Can Groups Engaged in Different Learning Experiences Be Started and Maintained?

The key to managing multiple learning experiences is to have clear directions that all students understand and clear routines that are well understood and practiced. Children know that they are expected to be engaging in learning and that they are respected members of the learning community.

Managing a classroom of elementary students all engaged in different learning experiences may seem like a daunting task. However, by creating some basic procedures, teaching those procedures to students, and practicing them at the beginning of the school year, building a classroom culture of differentiated learning can be a success! Often, students working either individually or in small groups will have questions as they are working, and they may engage in conversation about the learning task. These five practical tips can help a classroom teacher manage a differentiated learning environment:

- One basic requirement is to create a classroom climate of learning collaboratively; in this type of atmosphere, students can be encouraged to ask a partner or group member for help on a question.

- A second suggestion is to create some practiced norms for getting help from a teacher. The most common signal is hand raising, but other signals such as posting a question mark sticker or a stop sign (indicating the teacher should stop there) on a desk can work effectively as well without adding additional noise. Students may also have a two-sided card on their desk. Putting the predetermined color side facing up signals the teacher to stop by when he is available. This type of signal allows the child to keep on learning, whereas raising one's hand stops learning as the child waits for help.

- A third tip is to use the help of all adults in the classroom effectively and efficiently, including volunteers, collaborating teachers, university observers, and others. For this to work effectively, all adults must be aware of the various learning experiences students are engaging in and appropriate ways to help. The regular classroom teacher should create an expectation that, if appropriate, all adults in the classroom are to be actively supporting student learning. No opportunities to help are missed.

- Possibly the easiest suggestion, but one that is often overlooked, is to make sure that all student directions are clear. Many student questions are requests for clarifications about what to do or procedural questions about getting started or using resources. As students work on different tasks, make sure each task has clear, written instructions. These instructions could be individually typed on personal agendas, stapled in folders, labeled on learning centers, or clearly written on the board. Clear written directions ensure that all students are aware of their specific requirements and can begin to monitor their own progress. Following instructions and self-monitoring progress are routines to be taught and practiced throughout the year.

- Students should know that they are to save their questions until the teacher has finished working with a small group. Timing is important, and children save their learning time by using something like the two-colored card or stop sign mentioned earlier.

What Happens When Students Finish at Different Times?

Students should have clear directions for what they are to do when they complete any learning task. Having an agenda or written menu of the day's or week's expectations (learning experiences) prepares the student for what to do next and, hopefully, diminishes the need for a student to rush through one task as there are other learning experiences to enhance learning for each student. Students should know where to go in the room (a center or specific location) to get written instructions when they complete a learning experience or teachers can provide written directions in a folder at the students' desks. Students should always have anchor activities to which they can move when they have completed their learning experiences. These anchor activities focus on important learning outcomes and are engaging.

What Are Some Routines and Procedures That Must Be Established and Practiced Early in the Year?

In order for a differentiated classroom to run smoothly, it is important to invest some time at the beginning of the school year to teach and practice procedures and routines. Doing so will save time: both the teacher's time and learners' time. In a differentiated classroom on any given day, students may be working on different assignments, using various classroom resources, working individually and in small- or large-group settings, or meeting one-on-one with teachers. Procedures and routines are critical to manage this successfully. The following are some procedures that should be developed, modeled, and practiced early in the year; these procedures will be different based on classroom space, age of students, and individual teacher preferences.

Getting into groups. The teacher has a plan for the day for grouping so children know if they will be getting into pairs, triads, reading groups, math groups, or any other configuration. Ideally, charts or posters are placed throughout the room indicating whose desk or table goes where. Each child knows his role in creating that particular learning environment. Practicing these different groupings is similar to a theater production. What happens on stage is only part of the production. When the curtain closes between scenes, each actor or tech person is responsible for placing a certain piece of furniture or putting a prop exactly where it needs to be for an actor to use it on stage. Oftentimes stage managers place spike marks (i.e., tape) on the stage to indicate furniture or set placement. The same would work well in the classroom, perhaps using different colored tape for the different arrangements. Of course, these colors would be indicated on charts or posters guiding the child.

Turning in papers. Although there is no right or wrong way to turn in assignments, minimizing the time and any confusion as to how to do so should be the priority. The place to put completed assignments likely will be different from the place to put assignments on which the children will continue to work. In a classroom in which there are hanging folders, baskets, or other places for individuals to put their work, there may be a color-coded system of folders for assignments in reading, math, science, or social students. The teacher will organize and implement the system. The success of the system will depend upon communicating what to do and how to do it and then practicing to ensure that everyone understands what to do. That will save lots of questions as the year gets started. From then on, the expectation is that children will follow the system for turning in assignments.

Organizing assignments. A color-coded set of folders would provide a way to organize assignments in different content areas. Perhaps a different system would be to organize assignments at various centers in the room—reading center, writing center, math center, or any other center that is important for your curriculum.

Organizing make-up work. Within the classroom there needs to be one place where children go to "catch up" on assignments they missed due to absences. Likely, that missed work will be turned in wherever other assignments are to be turned in. Doing so keeps the system simple and easy for children to remember what to do. Teachers should be sure to include instructions plus copies of handouts used.

Getting and returning supplies. All children should know the location of all supplies that they may need. Math manipulatives, for example, will always be in the math center or in a particular place in the room. Likewise with other supplies—they will always be in a certain location in the room. Those locations will be dictated by the individual teacher's room and layout. Not only should these areas be clearly labeled, but children also should practice getting and returning supplies to where they are stored. Children also can assume roles on a weekly basis such as getting supplies needed for a learning activity, making sure that a center is neat, and replenishing any needed supplies.

Transitioning between activities. Periods of transition fill the day in an elementary school, and they certainly characterize a classroom in which learning experiences are differentiated. Routines need to be automatic and carried out in a manner that is respectful of children. The goal is to have children responsible for their own behavior because they know it is the right thing to do. Teachers encourage children to take charge of their own learning.

Arrival in the classroom in the morning is the first transition of the day—transitioning from home to school. Having something for the children to do and think about helps them settle in for a day of learning. Likewise, as they transition to afterschool activities, they may complete learning slips to reflect on what they have learned in a particular content area or learning experience and what questions they have as the result of the learning that day.

Other transitions occur as children switch from one content area or learning experience to another. For example, if reading occurs with different groups based on levels of reading, all children need to know the routine. If group A reads with the teacher first, then groups B and C need to know to get their reading materials and work independently until the teacher works with their group. All children need to know procedures that must be followed, such as not asking questions of the teacher while she is working directly with another small group.

Another transition point is getting ready to leave the room for time in the library or with another specials teacher (art, music, physical education, or foreign language) or to go to lunch. Lining up readily is an important routine to have in mind. Every procedure, including lining up, needs to show respect for the children.

Often, it is effective to give students a 5-minute warning that the task is ending and another learning experience is beginning. This affords students the opportunity to jot down final thoughts to jog their memory when they return to the task. It also signals them to go into transition mode—whether that is putting up supplies, turning in assignments, making an exit slip, or doing something else particular to the lesson.

How Is Progress Tracked?

Because continuous progress is one of the goals in a differentiated classroom, it is imperative to have a system to record progress. Likely, the system for record keeping is done on a computer. Recording letter grades does not communicate what is being learned in the same way that a description of learning does. Descriptive feedback and examples of work are important ways to communicate progress to children and to parents. Children and parents need to see examples of their learning, whether it is with writing samples, being able to solve math problems, or reading for understanding. Student products provide another source of evidence of what the child is able to understand and do, showing mastery of content and skills.

Communicating learning results to children and parents is essential in gaining support for differentiated learning experiences in a classroom.

What Makes Students Do Quality Work?

Two components must be in place to get students to do quality work. It is important that the work is worthy and that students have rubrics for products to guide their work on assignments or projects.

Children cannot thrive on busy work. The learning experiences must build in significant content and levels of thinking that challenge the child or group of children. Learning experiences that are matched to students' readiness to learn, interests in the content and in general, and learning profiles are likely to spark diligence and create quality learning.

Providing rubrics gives students a guide that includes the critical components necessary to complete a quality product. Roberts and Inman (2009a) created the Developing and Assessing Products (DAP) Tool as a way to assess student products in a consistent way based on four components: content, presentation, creativity, and reflection. It is a protocol that lets teachers use it consistently and with all products. Examples include Tiers 1, 2, and 3, and DAP Tools for posters, PowerPoints, collages, presentations, masks, interviews, movies, and much more. Several websites provide examples of prepared rubrics as well as places for educators to customize their own rubrics, including:

- http://rubistar.4teachers.org/
- http://www.schrockguide.net/assessment-and-rubrics.html

Providing choice of assignments based on learner profile or interest whenever possible also motivates students to produce quality work. See Chapter 8 for examples of differentiated learning experiences.

How Are Responsibilities Shared With a Collaborating Teacher?

There are three requirements for effectively sharing responsibility with a collaborating teacher. The first is that both the classroom teacher and the collaborating teacher must commit to the belief that all students can and will make continuous progress and that both teachers share responsibility to ensure that learning is the focus in the classroom. The second critical component is communication; either in a common planning time or in conversations before or after school, it is important that the collaborating teacher work with the classroom teacher to understand the standard and learning target, to plan learning experiences appropriate for all students (although the learning experiences will vary as they are matched to readiness, interests, and learner profile), and to help implement those experiences. The third requirement is the expectation that both teachers are actively involved in the learning experiences taking place in the classroom and are available and accessible to students as needed.

How Could Volunteers Facilitate Learning in a Differentiated Classroom?

The key to integrating classroom volunteers effectively into a differentiated classroom involves clear expectations and effective communication. First, it is important that volunteers know what is expected of them each visit. An initial orientation should outline expectations for the different tasks and responsibilities. For instance, one day they may be needed to create materials for learning centers, but the next day they may be needed to read one-on-one with students working on fluency or allowing advanced readers to read for expression. Their connection with students and willingness to work with small groups of students can make a huge impact on student learning. However, it is the teacher's responsibility to make those expectations clear to volunteers each day. Second, effectively communicating the purpose of the lesson (i.e., standard, learning targets, or skills) helps the volunteers know what the students are working on and how they can contribute to helping students master skills and/or content. Based on the volunteers' areas of expertise and comfort levels in working with students, they can be a huge asset to the classroom and facilitate student learning.

How Are Specials Teachers Integrated Into a Differentiated Classroom?

Specials teachers (such as art or music teachers) can make a huge impact on student learning in a differentiated classroom as they can extend or deepen the learning by helping students make connections. Whether in library, art, physical education, or music, connecting content learned in their regular classroom with learning experiences in their specials rotations makes a powerful learning experience for all students. One critical component is planning. For intentional curriculum connections to occur, principals and teachers must make a commitment to plan together and integrate standards for the various subjects. For instance, music and art teachers' expertise can be a huge asset to fifth-grade teachers exploring Colonial America. What a great way to explore Colonial life through the music, art, or dance of the period! Specials teachers should be included in all aspects of planning and implementing a standards-based K–5 curriculum.

A second critical piece is ongoing communication. As specials teachers work with students each week, it is important that they stay abreast of the units being taught in each grade level, so they can extend that learning and show applications in their respective content areas. Not only is knowing the content critical, but so is knowing the learners. Communicating about students' progress, mastery of learning targets, emotional and behavioral concerns, and special interest areas can make specials teachers a powerful part of the team that makes learning meaningful for all students. Intentional time either in faculty meetings, professional learning community (PLC) meetings, or grade-level team meetings is critical for this communication to happen.

How Can It Be Determined That Each Student Is Learning?

Ongoing assessment is the key to knowing that each child is learning. Formative assessment begins with preassessment, so the teacher knows the starting point for each child in terms of content and skills. But assessment must continue with other types of formative assessment. Checks of reading skill development as well as checks of concept understanding in math, science, and social studies can be made on charts, through anecdotal records, in performances (such as reading, speaking, designing), or in many other ways. Photographs (phones are handy for doing this) document products as do product assessments, whether with the DAP Tool or using rubrics. Assessment must be targeted to key indicators that learning outcomes are being reached or extended if they have already been attained. Continuous progress means that learning targets are moved on an ongoing basis to ensure that every child is learning every day in school.

Concluding Comments

Classroom management strategies set the stage for a classroom that accommodates children engaging in a variety of learning experiences that match their readiness to learn, interests, and learning profiles. Management strategies are in place and followed day by day. Procedures and routines are in place early in the school year. Classroom climate sets the tone of respect for children working together as a learning community and for the importance of all children learning on an ongoing basis.

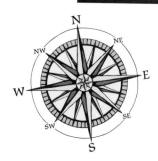

Survival Tips

- Be ready at the beginning of the school year to establish a climate that respects diversity and promotes all children learning on an ongoing basis.

- Establish routines and procedures early in the year and practice them until they are followed effortlessly.

- Don't expect all children to be doing the same thing at the same time. They come to learning experiences with a range of readiness and interests, no matter the learning outcome.

Survival Toolkit

- Tomlinson, C. A. (2001). *How to differentiate instruction in mixed-ability classrooms* (2nd ed.). Alexandria, VA: Association for Supervision and Curriculum Development. This book shows teachers how to use students' readiness levels, interests, and learning profiles to differentiate instruction.

- Tomlinson, C. A., & Imbeau, M. (2010). *Leading and managing a differentiated classroom.* Alexandria, VA: Association for Supervision and Curriculum Development. In their book, Tomlinson and Imbeau share practical information on managing the differentiated classroom.

- Setting the Stage for Differentiation (http://www.ascd.org/publications/educational-leadership/feb12/vol69/num05/Setting-the-Stage-for-Differentiation.aspx): Cindy Massicotte, a veteran teacher, wrote this article on differentiation.

11 A Differentiation Fable and Concluding Thoughts

Fable Contributed by Mandy Simpson

Key Question

- What lessons can animals illustrate about differentiation?

Once upon a time, three students—Frog, Zebra, and Lion—entered three different speech and debate classes. They worked hard as school began, and several things became apparent.

Frog felt self-conscious about the croaks in his speech but enjoyed reciting poetry written by himself or others. Lion tried very hard to control his boisterous roar by using facts and figures to support his opinions, and Zebra appeared embarrassed about her stripes except when surrounded by the intricate designs in her sketches and paintings.

After a few days of preliminary activities, the three classes began in earnest.

In order to be fair to everyone, Frog's teacher gave each student identical assignments and evaluations for every lesson. Lion's teacher did the same, believing the students would feel united by his "one for all" curriculum. Zebra's teacher, however, chose to give students varied projects and assessments.

After several months of school, Frog's croaking had grown worse with his nerves. He stumbled during the informative speech about another country, only

Figure 38. "One for all" curriculum. Illustration by J. W. Bellemere.

remembering which authors lived there, and he received poor marks on his ex-temporaneous speech because it came out in heroic couplets. Students who ex-celled in public speaking like Cockatiel earned top grades without much effort, which Frog didn't find fair at all.

Lion wasn't faring much better. Visuals were not allowed during his debate on white bread versus wheat bread, and he couldn't explain the ingredient lists and digestion rates without his pie chart and line graph. His teacher deducted points from another speech because he performed his own calculations rather than using all three research sources. Soon, Lion abandoned his facts and figures and simply roared until his debate opponents lost focus, which created an un-friendly classroom environment.

Zebra, however, was learning to respect the differences of students in her class. Her teacher allowed her to find creative ways to incorporate art into her speeches—like recording a podcast animated with her paintings and creating editorial cartoons for her debates. Zebra's evaluations looked different from her classmates because she had different strengths and weakness, and to get top marks, she had to work hard to improve upon both. Eventually, Zebra became confident in her speaking abilities and comfortable with her classmates. She gave her last speech on why zebras have stripes and used herself as the visual.

This fable illustrates what happens in classrooms in which teachers differentiate instruction and in which teachers do not differentiate. The latter often happens because the teachers believe it is fairer to treat everyone the same. Capitalizing on strengths (as Zebra's teacher believed) leads children to build confidence as they learn in an environment that is encouraging and respectful of differences. Frog, Lion, and Zebra could be Jack, Sally, and Jamal, and they represent children in classrooms across the country. In order for children to make continuous progress and to become lifelong learners, differentiation needs to become the standard practice in all elementary classrooms.

Hopefully, *Teacher's Survival Guide: Differentiating Instruction in the Elementary Classroom* can serve as a useful resource in making differentiation a standard practice. Effective differentiation does not happen overnight. It takes time, patience, and lots of trial and error. It takes careful examination and exploration of learners, discerning strengths and weaknesses, interests, learning profiles, and readiness levels. Effective differentiation starts with clear goals regarding who is being taught what in which manner and why—attention must be paid to content, process, product, and assessment and matching those appropriately to learners. It takes conscientiously establishing a healthy, respectful classroom culture for differentiation—one that celebrates diversity; promotes excellence, high expectations, and risk taking; nurtures a community of learners; and strives for excellence in teaching. It takes having a rich repertoire of strategies, knowing that some practices work well with some students and content while other strategies are more effective with others. And it takes organization, practiced classroom routines, and procedures that simplify the learning process. Yes, differentiation is a tall order, but it is the right thing to do for children.

References

Adams, C. M., & Pierce, R. L. (2011). *Differentiation that really works: Strategies from real teachers for real classrooms (grades K–2)*. Waco, TX: Prufrock Press.

American Association of School Librarians. (2007). *Standards for the 21st-century learner*. Retrieved from http://www.ala.org/aasl/guidelinesandstandards/learningstandards/standards

Anderson, L. W., & Krathwohl, D. R. (Eds). (2001). *A taxonomy for learning, teaching, and assessing: A revision of Bloom's taxonomy of educational objectives* (Abridged ed.). New York, NY: Longman.

Archambault, F. X., Jr., Westberg, K. L., Brown, S. W., Hallmark, B. W., Emmons, C. L., & Zhang, W. (1993). *Regular classroom practices with gifted students: Results of a national survey of classroom teachers* (Research Monograph 93102). Storrs: University of Connecticut, The National Research Center on the Gifted and Talented.

Armstrong, T. (2000). *Multiple intelligences in the classroom* (2nd ed.). Alexandria, VA: Association for Supervision and Curriculum Development.

Beasley, J. (2009, July). *Establishing classroom routines that support the differentiated classroom.* Presentation at the Association for Supervision and Curriculum Development Conference, Houston, TX.

Black, P., & Wiliam, D. (1998). Assessment and classroom learning. *Assessment and Education: Principles, Policy and Practice, 5*(1), 7–75.

Bloom, B. S. (Ed.). (1956). *Taxonomy of cognitive objectives: The classification of educational goals. Handbook I: Cognitive domain.* New York, NY: Longman.

Calkins, L. M., Montgomery, K., & Santman, D. (1998). *A teacher's guide to standardized reading tests: Knowledge is power.* Portsmouth, NH: Heinemann.

Campbell, L., & Campbell, B. (1999). *Multiple intelligences and student achievement: Success stories from six schools.* Alexandria, VA: Association for Supervision and Curriculum Development.

Carr, M. A. (2009). *Differentiation made simple: Timesaving tools for teachers.* Waco, TX: Prufrock Press.

Cash, R. M. (2011). *Advancing differentiation: Thinking and learning for the 21st century.* Minneapolis, MN: Free Spirit.

Coil, C. (2004). *Standards-based activities and assessments for the differentiated classroom.* Marion, IL: Pieces of Learning.

Conklin, W. (2010). *Differentiation strategies for social studies.* Huntington Beach, CA: Shell Education.

Constitutional Rights Foundation. (2010). *Boston plays.* Retrieved from http://www.crfcelebrateamerica.org/index.php/holidays/4th-of-july/75-boston-plays

Council of Chief State School Officers' Interstate Teacher Assessment and Support Consortium. (2011). *Model core teaching standards: A resource for state dialogue.* Washington, DC: Author.

Costa, A. L., & Kallick, B. O. (2000). *Habits of mind: A developmental series.* Arlington, VA: Association for Supervision and Curriculum Development.

Curry, J., & Samara, J. (1991). *Product guide kit.* Austin, TX: Curriculum Project.

Dunn, R., & Dunn, K. (2010). *Dunn and Dunn learning style models.* Retrieved from http://www.learningstyles.net

Dweck, C. S. (2007). *Mindset: The new psychology of success.* New York, NY: Ballantine.

Dweck, C. S. (2012). Mindsets and malleable minds: Implications for giftedness and talent. In R. F. Subotnik, A. Robinson, C. M. Callahan, & E. J. Gubbins (Eds.), *Malleable minds: Translating insights from psychology and neuroscience to gifted education* (pp. 153–163). Storrs: University of Connecticut, The National Research Center on the Gifted and Talented.

Elementary and Secondary Education Act of 2002, Title IX, 20 U. S. C. § 9101 *et seq.*

Engine-Uity. (2005). *Product pouch 2.* Phoeniz, AZ: Author.

Farkas, S., & Duffett, A. (2008). Results from a national teacher survey. In T. Loveless, S. Farkas, & A. Duffett (Eds.), *High-achieving students in the era of NCLB* (pp. 49–82). Washington, DC: Thomas B. Fordham Institute.

Fay, J., & Funk, D. (1995). *Teaching with love and logic: Taking control of the classroom.* Golden, CO: Love and Logic Press.

Finn, C. E., Jr., & Petrilla, M. J. (2008). Foreward. In T. Loveless, S. Farkas, & A. Duffett (Eds.), *High-achieving students in the era of NCLB* (pp. 8–12). Washington, DC: Thomas B. Fordham Institute.

Fisher, D. C. (1917). *Understood Betsy.* New York, NY: Henry Holt.

Fisher, T. (2012, March 7). *Two seconds.* Retrieved from http://blogs.edweek.org/teachers/unwrapping_the_gifted/2012/03/two_seconds.html

Gallagher, S. A. (2009). Adapting problem-based learning for gifted students. In F. A. Karnes & S. M. Bean (Eds.), *Methods and materials for teaching the gifted* (3rd ed., pp. 301–330). Waco, TX: Prufrock Press.

Gardner, H. (1983). *Frames of mind: The theory of multiple intelligences.* New York, NY: Basic.

Gentry, M. (2012, February). *Student-identified exemplary teachers: Insights from talented teachers.* Keynote at the Annual Conference of the Kentucky Association for Gifted Education, Lexington, KY.

Gentry, M., Steenbergen-Hu, S., & Choi, B. (2011). Student-identified exemplary teachers: Insights from talented teachers. *Gifted Child Quarterly, 55,* 111–125. doi:10.1177/0016986210397830

Ginott, H. G. (2003). *Between parent and child* (Revised and updated by Alice Ginott & H. Wallace Goddard). New York, NY: Three Rivers Press. (Original work published 1965)

Grigorenko, E. L., & Sternberg, R. L. (1997). Styles of thinking, abilities, and academic performance. *Exceptional Children, 63,* 295–312.

Heacox, D. (2002). *Differentiating instruction in the regular classroom.* Minneapolis, MN: Free Spirit.

Heacox, D. (2009). *Making differentiation a habit: How to ensure success in academically diverse classrooms.* Minneapolis, MN: Free Spirit.

Hewitt, K. K., & Weckstein, D. K. (2011). *Differentiation is an expectation: A school leader's guide to building a culture of differentiation.* Larchmont, NY: Eye on Education.

Jensen, E. (1998). The g factor and the design of education. In R. J. Sternberg & W. M. Williams (Eds.), *Intelligence, instruction, and assessment: Theory into practice* (pp. 111–132). Mahwah, NJ: Lawrence Erlbaum.

Jones, F. (2007). *Tools for teaching: Discipline, instruction, motivation.* Santa Cruz, CA: Fredric H. Jones & Associates.

Karnes, F. A., & Stephens, K. R. (2009). *The ultimate guide for student product development & evaluation* (2nd ed.). Waco, TX: Prufrock Press.

Kettle, K. E., Renzulli, J. S., & Rizza, M. G. (1998). Products of mind: Exploring student preferences for product development using My Way . . . An Expression Style Inventory. *Gifted Child Quarterly, 42,* 48–61. Retrieved from http://www.gifted.uconn.edu/sem/exprstyl.html

Kuhner, J. (2008). *High achieving students in the era of NCLB.* Retrieved from http://www.nagc.org/uploadedFiles/News_Room/NAGC_Advocacy_in_the_News/In%20a%20Nutshell%20(fordham).pdf

Lovelace, M. K. (2005). Meta-analysis of experimental research based on the Dunn and Dunn model. *Journal of Educational Research, 98,* 176–183.

Marzano, R. J., Pickering, D., & McTighe, J. (1993). *Assessing student outcomes: Performance assessment using the dimensions of learning model.* Alexandria, VA: Association for Supervision and Curriculum Development.

National Association for Gifted Children. (2010). *NAGC Pre-K–Grade 12 Gifted Education Programming Standards: A blueprint for quality gifted education programs.* Washington, DC: Author.

National Council for Accreditation of Teacher Education. (2008). *Professional standards for the accreditation of teacher preparation institutions.* Washington, DC: Author.

National Governors Association Center for Best Practices, & Council of Chief State School Officers. (2010a). *Common Core State Standards for English Language Arts.* Retrieved from http://www.corestandards.org/the-standards

National Governors Association Center for Best Practices, & Council of Chief State School Officers. (2010b). *Common Core State Standards for Mathematics.* Retrieved from http://www.corestandards.org/the-standards

National Research Council. (2012). *Education for life and work: Developing transferable knowledge and skills in the 21st century.* Washington, DC: National Academies Press.

New Teacher Center. (2011a). *TELL Colorado results details* (Data file). Retrieved from tellcolorado.org/reports/detailed.php?stateID=co

New Teacher Center. (2011b). *TELL Kentucky, detailed survey results.* Retrieved from http://tellkentucky.org/reports/detailed.php?stateID=KY

New Teacher Center. (2011c). *TELL Maryland, detailed survey results.* Retrieved from http://tellmaryland.org/reports/detailed.php?stateID=MD

New Teacher Center. (2011d). *TELL Tennessee, detailed survey results.* Retrieved from http://www.telltennessee.org/reports/detailed.php?stateID=TN

New Teacher Center. (2012a). *North Carolina: Teacher Working Conditions Initiative, detailed results.* Retrieved from http://ncteachingconditions.org/reports/detailed.php?stateID=NC

New Teacher Center. (2012b). *TELL Mass, detailed survey results.* Retrieved from http://tellmass.org/reports/detailed.php?stateID=MA

Partnership for 21st Century Skills. (2009). *Framework for 21st century learning.* Retrieved from http://www.p21.org/overview/skills-framework

Partnership for 21st Century Skills. (2011). *21st century readiness for every student: A policymaker's guide.* Tucson, AZ: Author.

Plucker, J. A., Burroughs, N., & Song, R. (2010). *Mind the (other) gap!: The growing excellence gap in K–12 education.* Bloomington, IN: Center for Evaluation and Education Policy.

Prensky, M. (2001). Digital natives, digital immigrants. *On the Horizon, 9*(5), 1–6. Retrieved from http://www.marcprensky.com/writing/Prensky%20 -%20Digital%20Natives,%20Digital%20Immigrants%20-%20Part1.pdf

Rakow, S. (2012). Helping gifted learners soar. *Educational Leadership, 69*(5), 34–40.

Riordan, R. (2005). *The lightning thief.* New York, NY: Disney Hyperion Books.

Roberts, J. L., & Boggess, J. R. (2011). *Teacher's survival guide: Gifted education.* Waco, TX: Prufrock Press.

Roberts, J. L., & Boggess, J. R. (2012). *Differentiating instruction with centers in the gifted classroom.* Waco, TX: Prufrock Press.

Roberts, J. L., & Inman, T. F. (2009a). *Assessing differentiated student products: A protocol for development and evaluation.* Waco, TX: Prufrock Press.

Roberts, J. L., & Inman, T. F. (2009b). *Strategies for differentiating instruction: Best practices for the classroom* (2nd ed.). Waco, TX: Prufrock Press.

Roberts, J. L., & Roberts, R. A. (2009). Writing units that remove the learning ceiling. In F. A. Karnes & S. M. Bean (Eds.), *Methods and materials for teaching the gifted* (3rd ed., pp. 189–221). Waco, TX: Prufrock Press.

Robinson, K. (2011). *Out of our minds: Learning to be creative* (2nd ed.). Chichester, West Sussex, UK: Capstone.

Shepard, L, Hammerness, K., Darling-Hammond, L., & Rust, F. (2005). Assessment. In L. Darling-Hammond & J. Bransford (Eds.), *Preparing teachers for a changing world* (pp. 275–326). San Francisco, CA: John Wiley & Sons.

Silver, H. F., Strong, R. W., & Perini, M. J. (2000). *So each may learn: Integrating learning styles and multiple intelligences.* Alexandria, VA: Association for Supervision and Curriculum Development.

Smutny, J. F., & Von Fremd, S. E. (2010). *Differentiating for the young child: Teaching strategies across the content areas.* Thousand Oaks, CA: Corwin Press.

Stanley, J. C. (2000). Helping students learn only what they don't already know. *Psychology, Public Policy, and Law, 6,* 216–222.

Stanley, T. (2012). *Project-based learning for gifted students.* Waco, TX: Prufrock Press.

Stephens, K. R., & Karnes, F. A. (2009). Product development for gifted students. In F. A. Karnes & S. M. Bean (Eds.), *Methods and materials for teaching the gifted* (3rd ed., pp. 157–186). Waco, TX: Prufrock Press.

Sternberg, R. J. (1985). *Beyond IQ: A triarchic theory of human intelligence.* New York, NY: Cambridge University Press.

Sternberg, R. J. (1997). What does it mean to be smart? *Educational Leadership, 55*(7), 20–24.

Sternberg, R. J., Torff, B., & Grigorenko, E. (1998). Teaching triarchically improves student achievement. *Journal of School Psychology, 90,* 374–384.

Stiggins, R. J., & Chappuis, J. (2012). *An introduction to student-involved assessment* for *learning* (6th ed.). Boston, MA: Pearson.

Teele, S. (1996). Redesigning the educational system to enable all students to succeed. *NASSP Bulletin, 80*(583), 65–75.

Tomlinson, C. A., Callahan, C. M., & Lelli, K. M. (1997). Challenging expectations: Case studies of high-potential, culturally diverse young children. *Gifted Child Quarterly, 41*(2), 5–17.

Tomlinson, C. A., & Imbeau, M. (2010). *Leading and managing a differentiated classroom.* Alexandria, VA: Association for Supervision and Curriculum Development.

Trail, B. (2012, April 14). *Twice exceptional children: Emphasizing 21st century skills and improving outcomes.* Paper presented at the annual meeting of the Council for Exceptional Children, Denver, CO.

Umphrey, J. (2010). *Toward 21st century supports: An interview with Linda Darling-Hammond.* Retrieved from http://www.nassp.org/Content.aspx?topic=60465

Vygotsky, L. S. (1978). *Mind in society: The development of higher psychological processes.* Boston, MA: Harvard University Press.

Wagner, T. (2008). *The global achievement gap.* New York, NY: Basic.

Ward, V. S. (1980). *Differential education for the gifted.* Ventura, CA: Ventura County Schools.

Ward, V. S. (1983). *Gifted education: Exploratory studies of theory and practice.* Manassas, VA: The Reading Tutorium.

Webb, N. L. (1999). *Alignment of science and mathematics standards and assessments in four states* (Research Monograph No. 18). Madison, WI: National Institute for Science Education.

Westberg, K. L., & Daoust, M. E. (2003). *The results of the replication of the Classroom Practices Survey replication in two states.* Retrieved from http://www.gifted.uconn.edu/nrcgt/newsletter/fall03/fall032.htm

Westphal, L. (2011). *Ready-to-use differentiated strategies: Grades 3–5.* Waco, TX: Prufrock Press.

Winebrenner, S. (1996). *Teaching kids with learning difficulties in the regular classroom: Ways to challenge and motivate struggling students to achieve proficiency with required standards.* Minneapolis, MN: Free Spirit.

Winebrenner, S. (2001). *Teaching gifted kids in the regular classroom: Strategies and techniques every teacher can use to meet the academic needs of the gifted and talented.* Minneapolis, MN: Free Spirit.

My Way ...

An Expression Style Inventory
K. E. Kettle, J. S. Renzulli, M. G. Rizza
University of Connecticut

Products provide students and professionals with a way to express what they have learned to an audience. This survey will help determine the kinds of products **YOU** are **interested** in creating.

My Name is: _____

Instructions:

Read each statement and circle the number that shows to what extent **YOU** are **interested** in creating that type of product. (Do not worry if you are unsure of how to make the product.)

		Not At All Interested	Of Little Interest	Moderately Interested	Interested	Very Interested
	Example: writing song lyrics	1	2	3	④	5
1.	writing stories	1	2	3	4	5
2.	discussing what I have learned	1	2	3	4	5
3.	painting a picture	1	2	3	4	5
4.	designing a computer software project	1	2	3	4	5
5.	filming & editing a video	1	2	3	4	5
6.	creating a company	1	2	3	4	5
7.	helping in the community	1	2	3	4	5
8.	acting in a play	1	2	3	4	5

My Way ...

An Expression Style Inventory

		Not At All Interested	Of Little Interest	Moderately Interested	Interested	Very Interested
9.	building an invention	1	2	3	4	5
10.	playing a musical instrument	1	2	3	4	5
11.	writing for a newspaper	1	2	3	4	5
12.	discussing ideas	1	2	3	4	5
13.	drawing pictures for a book	1	2	3	4	5
14.	designing an interactive computer project	1	2	3	4	5
15.	filming & editing a television show	1	2	3	4	5
16.	operating a business	1	2	3	4	5
17.	working to help others	1	2	3	4	5
18.	acting out an event	1	2	3	4	5
19.	building a project	1	2	3	4	5
20.	playing in a band	1	2	3	4	5
21.	writing for a magazine	1	2	3	4	5
22.	talking about my project	1	2	3	4	5
23.	making a clay sculpture of a character	1	2	3	4	5

		Not At All Interested	Of Little Interest	Moderately Interested	Interested	Very Interested
24.	designing information for the computer internet	1	2	3	4	5
25,	filming & editing a movie	1	2	3	4	5
26.	marketing a product	1	2	3	4	5
27.	helping others by supporting a social cause	1	2	3	4	5
28.	acting out a story	1	2	3	4	5
29.	repairing a machine	1	2	3	4	5
30.	composing music	1	2	3	4	5
31.	writing an essay	1	2	3	4	5
32.	discussing my research	1	2	3	4	5
33.	painting a mural	1	2	3	4	5
34.	designing a computer game	1	2	3	4	5
35.	recording & editing a radio show	1	2	3	4	5
36.	marketing an idea	1	2	3	4	5
37.	helping others by fundraising	1	2	3	4	5
38.	performing a skit	1	2	3	4	5
39.	constructing a working model	1	2	3	4	5
40.	performing music	1	2	3	4	5
41.	writing a report	1	2	3	4	5
42.	talking about my experiences	1	2	3	4	5

		Not At All Interested	Of Little Interest	Moderately Interested	Interested	Very Interested
43.	making a clay sculpture of a scene	1	2	3	4	5
44.	designing a multi-media computer show	1	2	3	4	5
45.	selecting slides & music for a slide show	1	2	3	4	5
46.	managing investments	1	2	3	4	5
47.	collecting clothing or food to help others	1	2	3	4	5
48.	role-playing a character	1	2	3	4	5
49.	assembling a kit	1	2	3	4	5
50.	playing in an orchestra	1	2	3	4	5

The End

My Way... A Profile

Instructions: Write your score beside each number. Add each <u>ROW</u> to determine <u>YOUR</u> expression style profile.

<u>Products</u>

						Total
Written	1. ___	11. ___	21. ___	31. ___	41. ___	___
Oral	2. ___	12. ___	22. ___	32. ___	42. ___	___
Artistic	3. ___	13. ___	23. ___	33. ___	43. ___	___
Computer	4. ___	14. ___	24. ___	34. ___	44. ___	___
Audio/Visual	5. ___	15. ___	25. ___	35. ___	45. ___	___
Commercial	6. ___	16. ___	26. ___	36. ___	46. ___	___
Service	7. ___	17. ___	27. ___	37. ___	47. ___	___
Dramatization	8. ___	18. ___	28. ___	38. ___	48. ___	___
Manipulative	9. ___	19. ___	29. ___	39. ___	49. ___	___
Musical	10. ___	20. ___	30. ___	40. ___	50. ___	___

Note. From "Products of Mind: Exploring Student Preferences for Product Development Using My Way . . . An Expression Style Inventory," by K. E. Kettle, J. S. Renzulli, and M. G. Rizza, 1998, http://www.gifted.uconn.edu/sem/exprstyl. html. Reprinted with permission of Joseph S. Renzulli.

About the Authors

Julia Link Roberts, Ed.D., is the Mahurin Professor of Gifted Studies at Western Kentucky University. She is the Executive Director of The Center for Gifted Studies and the Carol Martin Gatton Academy of Mathematics and Science in Kentucky. Julia is a member of the Executive Committee (Treasurer) of the World Council for Gifted and Talented Children and a board member of the Kentucky Association for Gifted Education and The Association for the Gifted (a division of the Council for Exceptional Children). Julia was honored with the 2011 Acorn Award given to an outstanding professor at a Kentucky college or university. She received the first David W. Belin NAGC Award for Advocacy. She is coauthor with Tracy Inman of *Strategies for Differentiating Instruction: Best Practices for the Classroom* (2009 Legacy Award for the outstanding book for educators in gifted education by the Texas Association for the Gifted and Talented) and *Assessing Differentiated Student Products: A Protocol for Development and Evaluation.* Julia and her daughter Julia Roberts Boggess coauthored *Teacher's Survival Guide: Gifted Education* and *Differentiating Instruction With Centers: Gifted Education.* She directs summer and Saturday programs for children and young people who are gifted and talented and teaches graduate courses in gifted education. Julia and her husband Richard live in Bowling Green, KY. They have two daughters, Stacy and Julia, and four granddaughters, Elizabeth, Caroline, Jane Ann, and Claire.

Tracy Ford Inman, Ed.D., is Associate Director of The Center for Gifted Studies at Western Kentucky University and is active on the state, national, and international levels in gifted education. She has taught English at the high school and collegiate levels, as well as in summer programs for gifted and talented youth. In addition to writing and cowriting several articles, Tracy has coauthored two books with Julia Roberts through Prufrock Press: *Strategies for Differentiating Instruction: Best Practices for the Classroom*, now in its second edition, and *Assessing Differentiated Student Products: A Protocol for Development and Evaluation*. Tracy and Julia received the Legacy Book Award from the Texas Association for the Gifted and Talented for *Strategies for Differentiating Instruction*. Tracy also was coeditor of *Parenting Gifted Children: The Authoritative Guide From the National Association for Gifted Children*, a compilation of the best articles in *Parenting for High Potential*, which won the Legacy Book Award in 2011.

About the Contributors

David Baxter has taught elementary school for 18 years. Currently, he works with high-ability students at the GEMS (Gifted Education in Math and Science) Academy in Bowling Green, KY. He has also taught several courses at the college level, including a math methods class for preservice teachers. David has presented on Web 2.0 technology for both the National Association for Gifted Children and the National Science Teachers Association. He earned a master's degree in folk studies at Western Kentucky University and completed his gifted endorsement in 2009.

Jana Kirchner, Ph.D., is an assistant professor in the School of Teacher Education at Western Kentucky University. Jana has 22 years of experience in education, which includes teaching high school history and English, serving as Social Studies Department Head/Curriculum Coordinator, being a social studies and literacy consultant for the Green River Regional Educational Cooperative, and serving as Executive Director of the Kentucky Council for Social Studies. She earned her Ph.D. in educational leadership (with an emphasis on curriculum and instruction) from the University of Louisville.

Jan Weaver Lanham, Ph.D., lives her passion for quality education for students through varied roles—principal, coordinator of gifted programs, gifted teacher, choral director, beginning band director, fine arts teacher, consultant, mentor, advocate for differentiation, and author. Named a Kentucky Hall of Fame Teacher, Jan has teaching experience at all grade levels, K–12, and in university teacher preparation programs. Jan serves on the board of the Kentucky Association for Gifted Education, having served two terms as state president, and serves on the Kentucky State Advisory Council for Gifted and Talented Education. She and her husband, Kevin, are the proud parents of three sons, Michael, Ryan, and Jonathan.

Mandy Simpson is the coordinator of communications and technology at The Center for Gifted Studies at Western Kentucky University. She joined the center's staff in January 2012, after spending most of her professional career in journalism. At The Center, Mandy combines the tasks she loves—web development, photography, multimedia production, social networking, and writing/reporting—with a mission she is passionate about: providing educational opportunities for gifted young people, rigorous professional development for teachers, and support for parents of gifted young people. Mandy graduated summa cum lade from Western Kentucky University with a bachelor's degree in news/editorial journalism and English literature.

Jennifer Smith is in her seventh year as an elementary teacher, after leaving her previous career in the construction industry. She earned a master's degree in teaching from Bellarmine University and completed her gifted endorsement through Western Kentucky University. She has experience working with at-risk students as a Title I math coach and has taught summer and Saturday enrichment classes for gifted and talented children. Jennifer has presented on the effective use of technology in the classroom for both the National Association for Gifted Children and the National Science Teachers Association. She is currently a teacher at the Gifted Education in Math and Science (GEMS) Academy, part of a grant-funded research partnership between Western Kentucky University and Warren County Public Schools in Bowling Green, KY.